Why Reading Is Hard
Viewers Guide

Nancy Clair

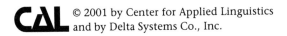

Printed in the United States of America
10 9 8 7 6 5 4 3 2 1

Why Reading Is Hard Viewers Guide
Editorial/production supervision: Carolyn Temple Adger, Lynn Fischer, and Deborah Kennedy
Interior and cover design: SAGARTdesign

ISBN 978-1-887744-67-6

This viewers guide was made possible by a grant from Carnegie Corporation of New York to Harvard University, and by the U.S. Department of Education's Office of Educational Research and Improvement under contract no. ED-99-CO-0008 to the Center for Applied Linguistics. The statements made and views expressed in this guide are solely the responsibility of the author and do not necessarily represent the opinions of the funders.

Acknowledgments

Thanks to staff and students of the Lowell Public Schools, Lowell, Massachusetts, especially Carmen Blasini, Deanna Farezadeh, Sharon Fennelly, Jean Franco, Christine Hickey, Paula Hutton, Mary Jane Kreegan, Ann O'Donnel, Deborah Romeo, Ted Rurak, Eileen Skovholt, and Tom Vennochi.

Permissions

Caterpillars, Bugs, and Butterflies, by Mel Boring, illustrated by Linda Garrow, © 1996 by NorthWord Press. Reproduced with permission.

Collecting Rocks and Crystals, by John Farndon, © 1999 by Quarto, Inc. Reproduced by kind permission of the copyright holder.

Icebergs and Glaciers, by Seymour Simon, © 1999 by Harper-Collins. Reproduced with permission.

Volcanoes, by Michael George, © 1993 by Creative Education. Reproduced with permission.

Welcome to the United States: A Guidebook for Refugees, © 1996 by Center for Applied Linguistics. Used with permission.

Photo used with permission from the Associated Press and Wide World Photos.

Arabic headline, *Al Hayat*, 21 June, 1999, used with permission.

Table of Contents

Overview

Teaching children to read is highly skilled work, and teaching children whose first language is not English is particularly challenging. As the number of students from non-English-speaking backgrounds grows, more and more teachers are presented with this challenge. Many of them may have had little or no preparation or support for understanding the literacy needs of the diverse array of students they teach.

Why Reading Is Hard—the video and this viewers' guide—is a resource for professional development. It is intended for teachers, professional development leaders, teacher educators, and others who seek to improve literacy instruction for all students. By demonstrating key elements of what's hard about reading, the video helps viewers discover some of the literacy skills that have become second nature to them as mature readers. Educators come away from watching it—more than once or twice, in order to get real insight—with new lenses for observing students' reading. Neither the video nor this guide recommends teaching strategies. Instead, they help teachers begin to ask useful questions about students' literacy so that they can select appropriate strategies for teaching. And they help teacher educators and professional developers figure out how they might better support classroom teachers through preservice and inservice education.

The video is based on a workshop at regional conferences on Improving America's Schools (IAS), presented by Professors Catherine Snow of Harvard University and Lily Wong Fillmore of the University of California at Berkeley. The purpose of this workshop was to spur thinking about the sorts of skills and knowledge that would contribute to improving language and literacy instruction in the schools. In this video, Doctors Fillmore and Snow point out some of the challenges that students face as they learn to read words and texts. They also show how teachers can analyze texts to discover the difficulties they can present. They emphasize that educators must know a great deal about language and literacy in order to support students' reading development.

This viewers guide provides information for using the video in professional development settings. A brief opening section describes ways of using the video and the other materials in this guide. Part One lists discussion questions and activities to extend viewers' learning. Part Two presents outlines for using the video as part of an ongoing study group. Part Three contains resources for the discussions and activities described in Parts One and Two: Arabic texts, students' readings, activities, a transcript of the video, questions and comments from the IAS conferences, guidelines for starting a study group, and background readings. Resources for further study, Internet sites, and a glossary are included.

How to Use the Video and Viewers Guide

To promote the reflection that helps teachers refine their classroom practice, professional development efforts must be clearly meaningful to teachers. Professional development for teachers must be connected to their students' learning. It must be interactive so that teachers can construct knowledge using each other's insights, and it must be long-term to ensure sustained attention to essential topics. The video and viewers guide encourage inquiry: Viewers are encouraged not only to learn new concepts but also to raise questions and seek answers that are relevant to the contexts in which they work.

Using *Why Reading Is Hard* in Study Groups

The video is designed for use in study group sessions that are part of a coherent professional development plan. Although the guide addresses leaders of a teacher study group, the video is also appropriate for use in study groups composed of professional development staff members or other educators who are developing professional knowledge and skills.

Field testing indicated that viewers found the video informative and concept-rich. Watching the video in a stand-alone session increased teachers' awareness of the complexities of literacy—and, consequently, of literacy instruction—but one viewing was not sufficient for deep understanding of concepts that can begin to change classroom practice. Likewise, viewing the video on its own, without referring to the materials in this guide, will deprive viewers of background information they need to be effective teachers of literacy.

Leading Study Groups

Study group sessions using *Why Reading Is Hard* can be led by experienced study group members, school district professional development staff, or consultants. Part One of this guide is targeted to facilitators who do not need a detailed guide to plan sessions and promote discussion. It provides discussion questions and extension activities to enhance study group members' understanding of the video content. Part Two is for facilitators who prefer a detailed guide for study group sessions. In either case, facilitators should adapt activities, questions, and session outlines based on the group's size, participants' experience working together, and their knowledge about literacy and diverse learners. A challenge in working on this topic is the range of beliefs that study group members may have. It will be important for the facilitator to achieve a balance of opinions and information—to create a climate in which individuals are free to express their views and to discuss research.

Integrating Viewing, Discussion, and Activities

Session facilitators can decide how to connect the video and the materials in this guide. The video can be viewed in full and the activities done later, or viewers may interrupt the video to do the activities. However, when the supplementary materials are used, this guide must be on hand before viewing begins because viewers will want to read texts that are shown in the video and reproduced in this guide.

Part One
Suggested Discussion Questions and Extension Activities

The video has three sections, each focusing on one dimension of the challenges inherent in reading:

• Reading words
• Reading texts
• The language of texts

The discussion questions and extension activities presented in Part One are keyed to the three sections of the video. They are meant to stimulate discussion and encourage inquiry. It is not necessary to address all of them. One role of the session facilitator is to work with other questions that arise and encourage viewers to address their own questions by reading and/or taking a close look at their classroom practice. Suggested outlines for study group sessions are presented in Part Two.

Pre-Viewing

These questions are intended to stimulate viewers' background knowledge in preparation for watching the video.

Questions

1. In your experience, what is hard about reading for native English speakers? For English language learners?
2. A major theme in *Why Reading Is Hard* is that teachers need to know a great deal about language and literacy in order to support students' reading development. What topics or ideas do you expect to encounter in the video? What do you expect to learn by viewing this video?
3. What is literacy? What questions do you have about literacy?

Viewing: Reading Words

A short lesson in Arabic allows viewers to experience what it is like to learn to read a new language. Prepare to view this section by turning to page 25 (Supplementary Materials A) where the Arabic texts begin and deciding how to integrate these texts with viewing the lesson. It will be important to stop the tape and work on the Arabic texts.

As you watch this section and the rest of the video, make a list of technical terms that are unfamiliar to you for discussion later.

Questions

4. Catherine Snow begins the first section of the video by explaining that she decided to study Arabic because she wanted to put herself in the position of an English language learner entering kindergarten or first grade. In what ways is she like a first grader? In what ways is she different?
5. Dr. Snow's pronunciation of Arabic letters and words shows that she does not have native-speaker proficiency in this language, which she began studying as an adult. What are the typical differences among child, adolescent, and adult learning of a new language? What are the implications of these differences for literacy instruction? (For more information on this topic, see Baker [1995] and Hakuta [1986] listed in the Further Study section.)
6. After learning the Arabic letters, can you read the headline that you saw in the video? It appears with a photograph on page 25.
7. How did you feel learning Arabic? Supplementary Materials E, Questions and Comments From the IAS Conferences (p. 67), presents discussion of the audience's experiences and questions about

the Arabic lesson. In what ways is the discussion relevant to your experience?

8. What connections can you make between your experience with Arabic and that of the English language learners you teach?

9. What is the *alphabetic principle* to which Dr. Snow refers? (See Glossary.) Why does she mention it?

Extension Activities

10. To extend understanding of why English words can be hard to read, work through "A Little Lesson in the Orthography of English," page 43. What did you learn from doing this exercise, and how can you use your insight?

11. Initiate a discussion with your students about the similarities and differences between their native languages and English, and any consequences for reading and writing that they're aware of. Talk with bilingual education staff, if they are not part of the study group. Report the results of your discussion to the study group at the next meeting. Discuss implications for instruction of what you have learned.

Viewing: Reading Texts

This section of the video concerns text comprehension. It shows examples of children, both native and non-native speakers of English, reading texts appropriate for their grade levels. The purpose of the examples is to learn from these children what is hard about the texts: Viewers will see demonstrations of reading comprehension, not examples of teaching. The children are elementary school students. Issues relevant to reading in earlier and later grades can be discussed in study groups.

Before you watch this section, turn to page 34 in Supplementary Materials B to locate texts from which students will be reading.

Questions

12. In the beginning of this video section, the narrator says that reading words is an important skill but that it does not lead automatically to comprehending text. Why? Give examples from the student interviews in the videotape or from your classroom experience that support your response.

13. If reading words does not lead automatically to comprehending text, what does that mean for literacy instruction? In what ways do you teach reading comprehension? How do you assess reading comprehension?

14. During the *Icebergs and Glaciers* segment, a conference participant raises a question about cognates. In what ways do you use English language learners' background knowledge or first language to encourage language transfer?

15. What observations or questions do you have about the students' reading ability in the *Icebergs and Glaciers* segment? In what ways are your reactions relevant to your own teaching?

16. The *Rocks and Crystals* segment refers to metaphorical language that the author uses in order to make meaning clear. However, the simile (the earth is like a perfectly boiled egg) does not seem to help the readers. Why?

17. What observations or new questions do you have about the students' reading ability in the *Rocks and Crystals* segment? In what ways are these relevant to your own teaching?

18. During the segment from *Caterpillars, Bugs, and Butterflies*, Georgiana says she knows the definition of a homophone for *mourning*, but she doesn't know what *mourning* means. What does that tell you about her understanding of the passage? What does it mean for instruction?

19. Using and building students' background knowledge is important for reading comprehension. In what ways do you use or build students' background knowledge related to texts they are reading? How do you know that what you are doing is sufficient?

20. What observations or new questions do you have about the students' reading ability in the *Caterpillars, Bugs, and Butterflies* segment? In what ways are these relevant to your own teaching?

21. At the IAS Conferences, participants discussed their experiences and raised questions about this section of the video. Read their discussion in Supplementary Materials E, (p. 70). In what ways is that discussion relevant to your teaching context?

22. What new questions do you have about reading texts? How will you find answers?

Extension Activities

23. With your colleagues, work on "A Little Lesson in Reading Text," page 46 in Supplementary Materials C. Be explicit about what you learn from this exercise and how you can use the insights for instructional purposes.

24. In your classroom, select a group of students to read a short passage from a text that is relevant to your curriculum and appropriate for the students' reading level. Then ask them about what they have read (use an interview format like those you saw in this section of the tape). Tape record and transcribe their responses. Use your

transcript in the next study group meeting to discuss questions that the experience has raised for you and what you have learned in terms of student comprehension, classroom instruction, and assessment.

25. Continue your discussion with your students about the similarities and differences between their native languages and English. With your students, begin a running list of cognates between English and your students' native languages. Help them locate dictionaries or other resources for determining whether the words are actually cognates.

Viewing: The Language of Texts

In this section, viewers will learn how academic language poses challenges for all students, including English language learners.

Questions

26. What are some characteristics of academic language, and how does that kind of English contrast with the language of social interaction? Use examples from the video, your classroom experience, and other venues. (For more information on academic English, see Cummins [1989] in the Further Study section.)

27. In the video, Catherine Snow and Lily Wong Fillmore advocate bringing content teachers and English teachers together to analyze texts. What benefits would this have for your teaching context? What would be the challenges? How could any challenges be overcome?

28. Before hearing the students discuss the *Volcanoes* passage, read the text (pp. 41-42). What aspects of the text do you think will be troublesome for monolingual students? For English language learners? Why?

29. What aspects of the *Volcanoes* text were actually troublesome for the students in the video? What instructional strategies could help students understand a passage like this?

30. In referring to academic texts, Lily Wong Fillmore says that *short* does not necessarily mean *easy*. What problems do simplified texts pose for students? Find a simplified text to support your response. (Check with an ESL teacher or in the school district's resource collection.)

31. Under what circumstances is simplifying text useful?

32. In what ways other than simplifying texts can you help your students gain access to them?

33. Lily Wong Fillmore says that many students, including English language learners, begin to experience serious reading difficulties in the fourth grade. What is it about the texts used at the fourth-grade level that makes them difficult for students? What assumptions are made about students' reading ability when they get to the fourth grade? What else is different at the fourth grade?

34. How does Dr. Fillmore recommend that vocabulary be taught? Do you find her recommendation useful? What does it mean for your classroom practice?

35. Dr. Fillmore recommends that teachers "unpack" texts with students, and she gives examples of unpacking with the *Volcanoes* text. What does "unpacking" mean? Why is this important? What are some ways to unpack academic texts with students?

36. At the IAS Conferences, participants discussed their experiences and raised questions about the language of texts. Read their discussion in Supplementary Materials E, page 71. In what ways is their discussion relevant to your teaching context?

37. What new questions do you have about the language of texts? How will you go about getting answers to your questions?

Extension Activities

38. Review the unpacked *Volcanoes* text in Supplementary Materials C, pages 50-52. Choose a text that is relevant to your setting and analyze it in the same way. You can do this alone or in a group, but be sure that you compare your analysis with that of at least one other colleague. After you have analyzed the text, discuss the following questions:
    a. What did you learn from the analysis?
    b. How does the analysis affect the way you would teach this text and assess student comprehension?
    c. What strategies can students use to assess their own reading comprehension? Do your students use these strategies? How do you know?

39. Choose a content area and examine textbooks in that area for Grades 3 and 4. What important differences do you see in the texts for these two grades in terms of visuals, format, types of activities, and language level?

40. Readability formulas usually involve calculating word difficulty (according to the frequency of their use or according to word length) and sentence complexity (according to the average number of words in a sentence). How are readability formulas relevant to what we know about simplified texts? (See Lily Wong Fillmore's comments in Supplementary Materials E, Questions and Comments from the IAS Conferences, p. 72.)

41. Examine your school's literature series to see if it provides measures of readability. Do these measures help you assess the appropriateness of the books and their contents for monolingual students and English language learners?

Post-Viewing

After the group has worked with each of the video sections, consider the video as a whole.

Questions

42. The pre-view questions asked you to predict the topics and ideas that you might see in the video. How close were your predictions to what you saw? Did you learn what you expected to learn?

43. The pre-view questions asked you to define literacy. Should you revise your definition?

44. The pre-view questions asked you what questions you had about literacy. Did you get answers to any of your questions? What new questions do you have as a result of viewing the video and discussing it? How will you locate answers to your questions?

Extension Activity

45. You were asked to list unfamiliar technical terms used in the video. Discuss the meanings of these terms with your colleagues, using the Glossary if necessary.

Part Two

Outlines for Using
the Video and Guide in Study Groups

Part Two suggests an approach to using *Why Reading Is Hard* in an already functioning study group. It outlines four 2-hour sessions in which group members watch the video, discuss the issues it raises, work on activities together, and plan follow-up. The outlines are designed for facilitators who want a somewhat detailed plan for using the video and supporting materials, but they are intended as guides rather than prescriptions for practice. Facilitators should adapt these outlines based on the needs of the study group.

Session One: Introduction

Objectives

- Introduce literacy as a topic for study, connecting it to the group's previous work and ongoing focus.
- Exchange beliefs and foundational knowledge about literacy.
- Raise questions for further study about literacy.
- Create preliminary plans and delegate responsibilities for the next study group session.

Pre-Viewing (15 minutes)

- Begin the session by telling group members that they will see a video entitled *Why Reading Is Hard.*
- Give the group background information about the video. Explain that it is divided into three sections: Reading Words, Reading Texts, and the Language of Texts. Stress that it is not about what teachers can do on Monday morning. (See page 2 for more information about the video.)
- Ask group members what they expect to see and learn from the video (pre-view questions 1-3, p. 6). Have group members write their answers so that they can revisit them later.
- Have group members discuss their responses in pairs or triads.
- Tell participants to turn to page 25 in the Supplementary Materials to find the texts that appear in the video.

Viewing (40 minutes)

- Ask group members to watch for what they've said they expect to see and to jot down technical vocabulary that they hear.
- Show the video.

Post-Viewing Discussion (40 minutes)

- Ask group members to respond to the post-view questions 42-45, page 11.
- Have group members discuss their responses in groups of three or four. Have one group member take notes on the group's definition of literacy, technical vocabulary, and new questions.
- Place three flip charts around the room and label them "definition of literacy," "technical vocabulary," and "new questions." Have the reporter for each group write responses on each chart based on the group discussion.
- In the large group, discuss the "definition of literacy" and "technical vocabulary" flip charts first. Respond to each other's questions. Refer to the Glossary (p.105), if necessary.

- Review the "new questions" flip chart. Are there similar questions? Discuss how the group might go about answering the questions.

Planning and Responsibilities for Next Study Group Meeting (25 minutes)

Decide as a group on activities to undertake for the next study group meeting. If appropriate, ask study group members to volunteer to facilitate all or parts of the next session. Suggested ideas for follow-on are listed below:

- Based on the issues and questions that emerged from discussion, the study group may want to look over the readings in Section G (p. 81) and select one to discuss during the meeting.
- Study group members may want to address one of the questions that emerged from their discussion. This may entail collecting classroom data/lesson plans, classroom observations, and/or analyzing texts. Data may be brought to the next meeting for discussion.
- Study group members may want to watch the video section by section. In preparation, all study group members should review Part One, Suggested Discussion Questions and Extension Activities (pp. 6-7), before the next session.

Outlines for study group meetings on the video sections follow.

Session Two: Reading Words

Objectives
- Review outstanding issues from the previous study group session.
- Experience learning a second language and relate that experience to literacy instruction for English language learners.
- Explore the differences among adult, child, and adolescent second language learning (optional).
- Plan for a classroom discussion about the similarities and differences between students' first languages and English (optional).
- Extend understanding of why English words can be hard to read (optional).
- Create preliminary plans and delegate responsibilities for the next study group session.

Discussion of Outstanding Issues from Previous Study Group Session

(This may take up to one hour if teachers are reporting on classroom data collection, discussing a reading, or raising an issue.)

- Review assignments, group responsibilities, and updates from previous study group session.

Pre-Viewing (15 minutes)
- Tell study group members that they will see the first section of the video *Why Reading Is Hard* again. In the section "Reading Words," viewers will experience a short lesson in Arabic.
- Ask the group what they think the purpose of experiencing an Arabic lesson is and how this relates to literacy practices.
- Ask the group how they think they will feel as they do the Arabic lesson.
- Have the participants turn to page 25 in the Supplementary Materials, where they will find the Arabic texts that appear in the video.

Viewing (15 minutes)
- Show the first section of the video, "Reading Words," pausing the tape to allow participants to work with the Arabic texts.

Post-Viewing Discussion (20 minutes)
- Ask group members to do a free write about how they felt learning Arabic and what insights they have regarding literacy practices for English language learners.
- Have group members compare responses in pairs or triads. (Refer to Supplementary Materials E, Questions and Comments from the IAS Conferences (p. 67) to compare study group members' reactions with those of workshop participants.)
- In the large group, ask group members for insights, questions, and comments.

Post-Viewing Discussion: Child, Adolescent, and Adult L2 Learning (25 minutes) (optional)
- Ask study group members to draw three columns on a sheet of paper and label them "Child Language Learner," "Adolescent Language Learner," and "Adult Language Learner."
- In pairs, have group members brainstorm differences in language learning for these age groups.
- In the whole group, discuss Question 5, Part One (p. 6), about child, adolescent, and adult second language learning. What are the typical differences among them? What are the implications for literacy instruction? Refer to Baker (1995) and Hakuta (1986) in the Further Study section.

Post-Viewing Discussion: Similarities and Differences Between Students' First Languages and English (25 minutes) (optional)

- Ask study group members to list the first languages of their students and talk about similarities and differences between their students' first languages and English. Use group members as resources.
- Brainstorm how teachers could plan to raise their own and their students' awareness of language differences and similarities (Reading Words Extension Activities, Question 11, p. 7).

Post-Viewing Discussion: Extend Understanding of Why English Words Can Be Hard to Read (25 minutes) (optional)

- In groups, work through "A Little Lesson in the Orthography of English" (Reading Words Extension Activities, Question 10, p. 43).
- In the whole group, discuss what you learned from doing this exercise and how your insights apply to literacy instruction for native-English speakers and English language learners. Decide whether group members want to learn more about reading words. One way to pursue this topic is to identify a group member or members who would like to read one of the resources listed under Further Study (p. 101), and lead a discussion of it.

Planning and Responsibilities for Next Study Group Meeting (15 minutes)

As a group, decide on activities for the next study group meeting. If appropriate, ask study group members to volunteer to facilitate all or parts of the next session. Suggested ideas for follow on are listed here:

- Based on the issues and questions that emerged from discussion, the study group may want to refer to Further Study, page 101. Study group members can select a reading to discuss during the next study group meeting.
- Study group members may want to address a question or issue that emerged from the discussion. This may entail collecting classroom data/lesson plans, classroom observations, and/or analyzing texts. This data can be brought to the next meeting for discussion.
- Study group members may want to report on a classroom discussion about the differences and similarities of students' first languages and English.
- Study group members may want to do the optional activities for this session.
- Study group members may decide to watch the next section of the video. In preparation, they should review Part One, Suggested

Discussion Questions and Extension Activities, pp.7-9, before the next session.

Session Three: Reading Texts

Objectives
- Review outstanding issues from previous study group session.
- Examine what can be hard about reading texts for both non-native and native English-speaking students.
- Apply insights in reflecting on literacy practice.
- Create preliminary plans and delegate responsibilities for the next study group session.

Discussion of Outstanding Issues from Previous Study Group Session
(This may take up to one hour if teachers are reporting on classroom data collection, discussing a reading, or raising an issue.)
- Review assignments, group responsibilities, and updates from previous study group session.

Pre-Viewing (10 minutes)
- Tell study group members that they will see the second section of *Why Reading Is Hard*. In this section, "Reading Texts," viewers will see elementary school students reading texts that are appropriate for their grade level.
- Ask the group to recall the kinds of difficulties that students had.
- Tell participants to turn to page 34 in the Supplementary Materials to locate the texts from which the students are reading.

Viewing (15-30 minutes)
- Show the "Reading Texts" portion of the video.
- When you see the texts' covers, pause the video, and have group members read the text and predict what will be difficult for students.

Post-Viewing Discussion (20 minutes)
- Ask group members to review their predictions for each reading passage.
- Ask group members to do a free-write: Were the predictions accurate? What was surprising about this video segment?
- Have group members compare responses in pairs or triads.

- In the large group, ask group members for insights, comments, and questions.
- Chart group members' questions and discuss responses (optional).

Post-Viewing Discussion: Part One, Discussion Questions 12-22 (35 minutes)

- Count off the group by fours. Divide the questions for this section so that each group discusses at least three of them. Ask one person in the group to take notes, jotting down new questions that arise.
- In the large group, have a spokesperson for each group report on one insight from the group discussion.

Planning and Responsibilities for Next Study Group Meeting (15 minutes)

Decide as a group what activities will follow for the next study group meeting. If appropriate, ask study group members to volunteer to facilitate all or parts of the next session. Ideas for follow-on are listed here:

- Based on the issues and questions that emerged from discussion, the study group may want to refer to Further Study, page 101. Study group members can select a reading to discuss during the next meeting.
- Study group members may want to address a question or issue that emerged from the discussion. This may entail collecting classroom data/lesson plans, classroom observations, and/or analyzing texts. This data can be brought to the next meeting for discussion.
- Study group members may want to work on "A Little Lesson in Reading Text" (Reading Texts Extension Activities, Question 23, p. 8).
- Study group members may want to report on a classroom discussion about the differences and similarities of students' first languages and English. (Reading Texts Extension Activities, Question 25, p. 9).
- Study group members may want to watch the final section of the video. In preparation, they should review Part One, Suggested Discussion Questions and Extension Activities, pages 9-11, before the next session. An outline for a session on that section follows.

Session Four: The Language of Texts

Objectives
- Review outstanding issues from the previous study group session.
- Explore the characteristics of academic language.
- Examine texts to predict what types of difficulties students may have and discuss implications for literacy instruction.

- Create preliminary plans and delegate responsibilities for the next study group session.

Discussion of Outstanding Issues from Previous Study Group Session

(This may take up to one hour if teachers are reporting on classroom data collection, discussing a reading, or raising an issue.)

- Review assignments, group responsibilities, and updates from the previous study group session.

Pre-Viewing (10 minutes)

- Tell study group members that they will see the third section of the video *Why Reading Is Hard*, "The Language of Texts." Viewers will learn how academic English poses challenges for students, including English language learners.
- On the board, write "Academic English is ...." Ask group members to finish the sentence. Discuss their responses.
- Have participants turn to page 40 in the Supplementary Materials to locate the text from which the student will be reading.

Viewing (15-25 minutes)

- Show the final section of the video. Ask group members to jot down characteristics of academic English mentioned in the video.
- Before the *Volcanoes* reading segment, stop the video and have group members read the text and predict what will be difficult for students. (optional)

Post-Viewing Discussion (15 minutes)

- Ask group members to discuss general reactions to this segment. What was surprising/affirming about this video segment?

Post-Viewing Discussion: Part One, Discussion Questions 26-37 (35 minutes)

- Count off the group by fours. Divide the questions so that each group discusses at least three questions. Ask one person in the group to take notes, jotting down new questions that arise.
- In the large group, have a spokesperson for each small group report on one insight from the group discussion.

Planning and Responsibilities for Next Study Group Meeting (15 minutes)

As a group, decide on activities for the next study group meeting. If appropriate, ask study group members to volunteer to facilitate all or parts of the next session. Suggested ideas for follow-on are listed here:

- Based on the issues and questions that emerged from discussion, the study group may want to refer to the list of readings, page 101. Study group members can select a reading to discuss during the next meeting.
- Study group members may want to address a question or issue that emerged from the discussion. This may entail collecting classroom data/lesson plans, classroom observation, and/or analyzing texts. This data can be brought to the next meeting for discussion.
- Study group members may want to analyze grade level texts, examine the differences between third and fourth grade texts, discuss readability formulas, or examine the school's literature series (The Language of Texts, Extension Activities, Questions 38-41, pp. 10-11).
- Study group members may want to review concepts from the video and discuss the post-viewing Questions 42-44 (p.11).

Part Three
Supplementary Materials

Part Three presents materials, many taken directly from the video, for use in study group activities and further study. Materials are shown in the order in which they appear in the video. Also included is the written transcript to assist in locating specific points and topics in the video. Other materials are referenced in Part One: Suggested Discussion Questions and Extension Activities.

THREE

Supplementary Materials

A. Arabic Texts

B. Students' Readings

C. Activities

D. Video Transcript

E. Questions and Answers from IAS Conferences

F. Guidelines for Starting a Study Group

G. Readings

Supplementary Materials

A. Arabic Texts

كلينتون ويلتسن يطويان صفحة كوسوفو

The Arabic Alphabet

Name of Letter	Final	Medial	Initial	Standing Alone
'Alif	هنا	تاب	أخ	ا
Baa'	كوب	لبن	بارع	ب
Taa'	تحت	كتب	تراب	ت
Th!aa'	مثلث	مثال	ثلج	ث
Jiim	خليج	نجح	جيش	ج
H'aa'	ملح	بحر	حبل	ح
Khaa'	مناخ	شخص	خرج	خ
Daal	سد	مدرس	دين	د
Thaal	بذ	هذا	ذاكرة	ذ
Raa'	بئر	ثري	رأي	ر
Zaay	طرز	تزوج	زيت	ز
Siin	شمس	مسجد	سمع	س
Shiin	مشمش	مشرق	شجرة	ش
Saad	لص	مصر	صمم	ص
Daad	نبض	فضل	ضغط	ض
Taa'	ربط	محطة	طعام	ط

Dh:aa'	محافظ	مظلة	ظريف	ظ
'Ayn	بجع	بعيد	عجل	ع
Ghayn	بلغ	ببغاء	غواصة	غ
Faa'	سقف	شفيق	فأر	ف
Qaaf	سبق	مقدمة	قارب	ق
Kaaf	سمك	سكر	كبير	ك
Laam	رمل	كلمة	لص	ل
Miim	علم	شمعة	مكان	م
Nuun	سمين	منبر	نحلة	ن
Haa'	سمعه	مهاجر	هبط	ه
Waaw	قبو	موت	وردة	و
Yaa'	يبكي	كبير	يد	ي

kaaf	ك
laam	ل
miim	م
nuun	ن
qaaf	ق

Kaaf

ك   كان كيس سكين شوكة سمك شباك   كو يكو يك

final   medial   initial

Laam

ل   لين ليرا لوز لوج كيلو نيل قول   لو يلو يل

Nuun

ن   نيل نير نور تنس كنغر بنت مين فرن   نو ينو ين

Qaaf

ق   قام قول قربان رقاقات نقانق ورق   قو يقو يق

إن التعليم متاح لكل شخص في الولايات المتحدة بغض النظر عن عمر الشخص أو عرقه أو دينه أو طبقته الاجتماعية. التعليم العام مجاني ويفرضه القانون على جميع الأطفال بين عمر **6** و **16** وقد يكون متاحا للأطفال بعمر أصغر أو أكبر حسب أنظمة المنطقة التعليمية المحلية. وللأبوين خيار آخر وهو تسجيل أبنائهم في مدارس خاصة وللكثير من هذه المدارس ارتباطات دينية إلا أن أجور التعليم فيها غالبا ما تكون باهظة. ويمكن أن يكون التعليم لما بعد المرحلة الإعدادية باهظا جدا.

In the United States, education is accessible to everyone, regardless of a person's age, race, religion, or social class. Public education is free and required by law for all children ages 6 to 16, and may also be available for children older or younger, depending on local school district regulations. Alternatively, parents may enroll children in private schools, many of which have religious affiliations, but tuition at these schools is often expensive. Beyond high school, education can be quite extensive.

From *Welcome to the United States: A Guidebook for Refugees*, p. 53, © Center for Applied Linguistics, 1996. Reprinted with permission.

إن التعليم متاح لكل شخص في الولايات

المتحدة بغض النظر عن عمر الشخص أو عرقه

أو دينه أو طبقته الاجتماعية. التعليم العام

مجاني ويفرضه القانون على جميع الأطفال بين

عمر 6 و 16 وقد يكون متاحا للأطفال بعمر

أصغر أو أكبر حسب أنظمة المنطقة التعليمية

المحلية. وللأبوين خيار آخر وهو تسجيل أبنائهم

في مدارس خاصة وللكثير من هذه المدارس

ارتباطات دينية إلا أن أجور التعليم فيها غالبا

ما تكون باهظة. ويمكن أن يكون التعليم لما

بعد المرحلة الإعدادية باهظا جدا.

امريكا   بالون   كوالا   ليمون

_____   _____   _____   _____

Supplementary Materials

B. Students' Readings

ICEBERGS AND GLACIERS

SEYMOUR SIMON

The thicker the glacier the faster it moves. That's because the greater weight of the glacier causes the crystals of ice to creep more rapidly. Also, a steep glacier will flow much more quickly than one on level land.

Temperature is a third factor that affects the speed of a glacier. The warmer the glacier the faster the ice moves because there is a greater amount of meltwater beneath the ice. In fact, scientists sometimes group glaciers together depending upon whether they are cold or warm. But even "warm" glaciers are still freezing.

Some glaciers move so slowly that you might not notice their movement for a long time. The cold Alaskan glaciers in this aerial photo creep downhill at only about six inches per *year*. But there are some steep, warm glaciers that flow more than one hundred feet a *day*.

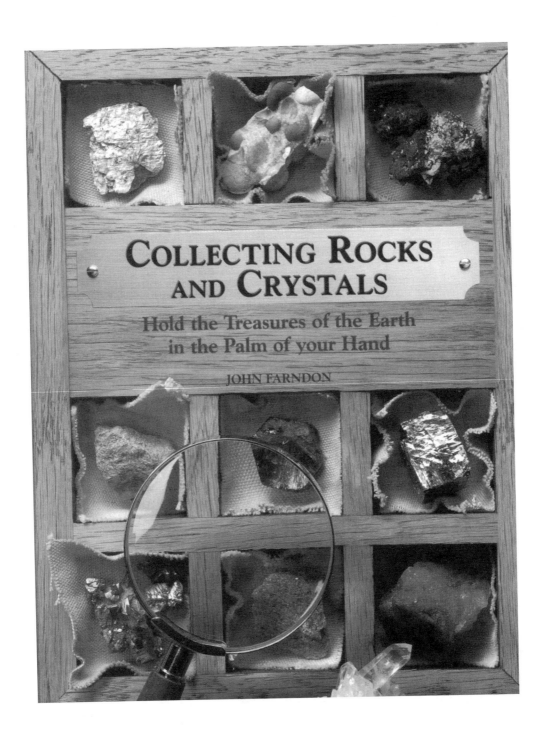

COLLECTING ROCKS
AND CRYSTALS

Hold the Treasures of the Earth
in the Palm of your Hand

JOHN FARNDON

Introducing Rocks and Crystals

ROCKS AND CRYSTALS are the raw materials of the Earth's surface—the material beneath every hill and valley, mountain and plain. Some are just a few million years old. Others are almost as old as the Earth.

What are rocks?

ROCKS ARE NEVER far beneath the ground. They are only exposed on the surface in a few places—such as bare rock outcrops, cliff faces and quarries. But dig down almost anywhere on the Earth's surface and you will come to solid rock before long.

Like the other smaller planets in the solar system, our world is made almost entirely from rock. The Earth is a bit like a perfectly boiled egg—with a semi-liquid yolk or "core," surrounded by a thick, soft layer called the mantle, and covered by a thin hard shell called the crust. The core in the very center is metal but the crust and mantel are made entirely from rock.

ROCKS AND MANKIND

No wonder, then, that rocks have played such an important part in mankind's history. Rocks were used by humans for their very first cutting tools, millions of years ago. At least three million years ago, early hominids (manlike creatures) were chipping the edge off hand-sized round pebbles, perhaps to use as weapons. Two million years ago, hominids began using flints to make two-sided hand-axes, which is why the first age of man is known as the Stone Age.

Later, clay was used to make pottery, and since then mankind has found an increasing variety of ways to use rocks. They can be broken up and reshaped to provide building materials for everything from cottages to cathedrals, harbor walls to roads. Certain minerals—the natural chemicals they are made from—can be extracted or processed to make a huge range of materials. All metals, such as iron, copper, and tin, come from minerals contained in rock. So do most

ROCK SOURCE *(below)*
One of the best places to see living rock is in quarries, where it is blasted and dug from the ground to provide building stone and other materials.

•6•

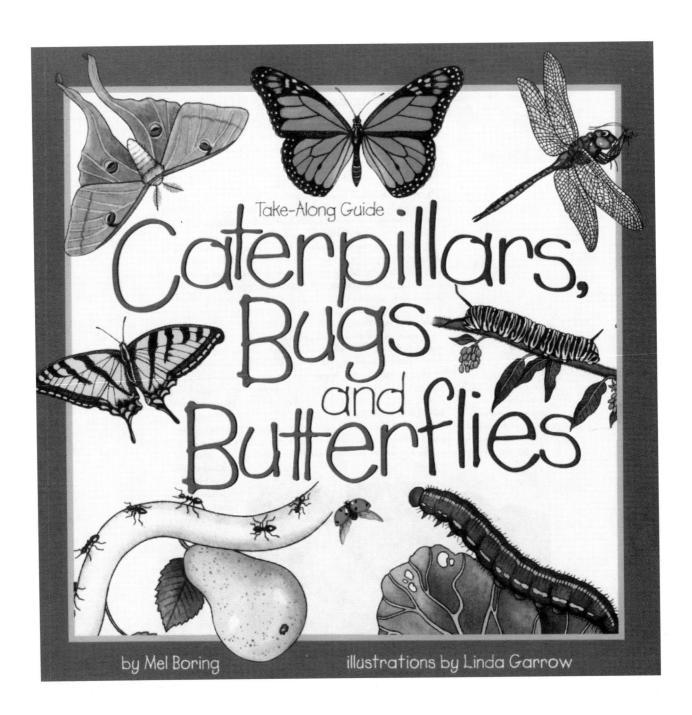

Take-Along Guide

Caterpillars, Bugs and Butterflies

by Mel Boring   illustrations by Linda Garrow

MOURNING CLOAK CATERPILLAR

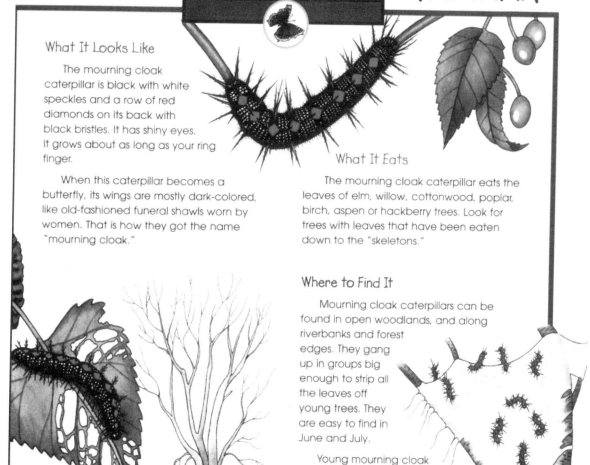

What It Looks Like

The mourning cloak caterpillar is black with white speckles and a row of red diamonds on its back with black bristles. It has shiny eyes. It grows about as long as your ring finger.

When this caterpillar becomes a butterfly, its wings are mostly dark-colored, like old-fashioned funeral shawls worn by women. That is how they got the name "mourning cloak."

What It Eats

The mourning cloak caterpillar eats the leaves of elm, willow, cottonwood, poplar, birch, aspen or hackberry trees. Look for trees with leaves that have been eaten down to the "skeletons."

Where to Find It

Mourning cloak caterpillars can be found in open woodlands, and along riverbanks and forest edges. They gang up in groups big enough to strip all the leaves off young trees. They are easy to find in June and July.

Young mourning cloak caterpillars hang out together in webs. If you disturb their web, they wiggle like dancers dancing.

10

From *Caterpillars, Bugs, and Butterflies,* by Mel Boring © 1996 by NorthWord Press
Reproduced with permission

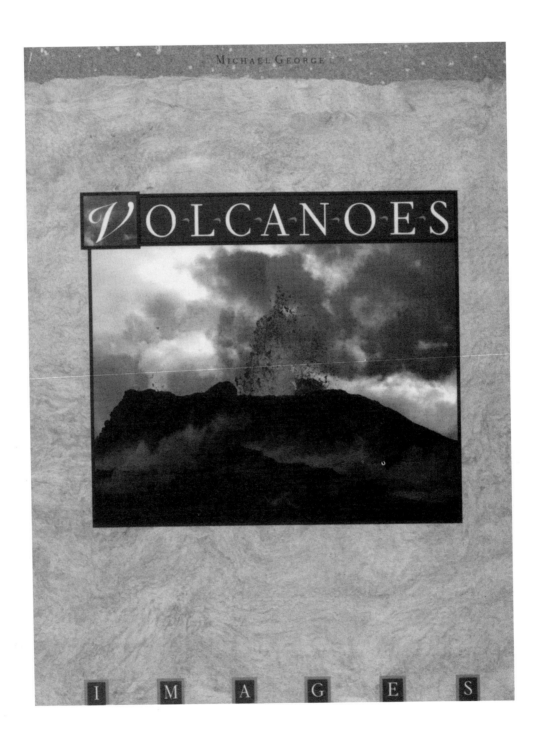

MICHAEL GEORGE

VOLCANOES

I M A G E S

10

Volcanoes that erupt regularly are known as *Active Volcanoes*. There are about six hundred active volcanoes on the Earth's surface. However, only fifty to sixty active volcanoes erupt in any given year.

Whether sitting in silence or erupting with violence, volcanoes have intrigued people for thousands of years. In an attempt to explain the immense power and unpredictable

Cotopaxi volcano in Ecuador.

From *Volcanoes*, by Michael George © 1993 by Creative Education
Reproduced with permission

11

behavior of volcanoes, our ancient ancestors created myths about evil gods that lived within volcanoes. When angered, the gods would display their fury with eruptions.

Today, scientists explain volcanoes without relying on angry gods. However, the true causes for *Volcanic Eruptions* are as fascinating as the ancient myths.

Heimaey volcano in Iceland.

From *Volcanoes,* by Michael George © 1993 by Creative Education
Reproduced with permission

Supplementary Materials

C. Activities

A Little Lesson in the Orthography of English
Catherine Snow

The orthography of English is deep. Consider the following sentence:

> Sayuhntists had fauwnd thuh djeen that hwen deefektiv kawzuhz thuh deebiluhteiting and awltuhmuhtli feituhl dizeez.

Different spellings can produce the same sound. The mapping between sound and spelling in English is hard to learn—considerably harder than for other European languages, for which children have mastered the basics of the alphabetic principle and can read pseudowords after only one year of instruction. English speakers don't score that well until they've had about three years of instruction.

Reading words that look familiar is much easier than reading words that are not familiar.

Exercise 1

Directions:
a. Cover columns B and C. Read the words in column A.
b. Cover columns A and C. Read the words in column B.
c. Cover columns A and B. Read the words in column C.

A	B	C
attack	peepuhl	buhndr
brew	laf	luhdj
brought	kahmpleks	veezayn
coffee	hol	mayuhnts
complex	tawkt	yol
design	wuhndr	grawt
dutiful	thru	uhhak
food	djuhdj	haufey
hole	uhtak	baf
judge	brawt	zeepuhl
laugh	deezayn	fru
people	dutuhfl	vud
science	fud	wahmpleks
talked	kawfey	kutuhfl
through	sayuhnts	nawkt

Which column was easiest to read? Which was hardest? Why?

Exercise 2

Which of the following sentences is/are hardest to read? Why?

A1. The government has not brought any charges against its prime suspect.
A2. The blutoricy has not chintimed any charges ablend its prime suspect.

B1. The new agency will supervise the nationwide network of laboratories.
B2. The new plungory will sumandeer the chroadsy maves of skuedles.

C1. According to the department's proposed regulations, the polygraph exams will be voluntary.
C2. Mergant min uda thrun's aiminfeldout durtas, ab exofeanoperald fluths ziplin gobune appuquary.

A Little Lesson in Reading Text

Catherine Snow

Lots of information must be available and even more inferred to read most texts.

1. **Answer the questions following these excerpts from a newspaper article** (*The Wall Street Journal*, June 11, 2001, p. 1). **Explain how you knew the answer, with reference to the text. Explain also what information outside the text you needed to answer the questions.**

Twelve years ago, Danny Bessette was a symbol of hope that a cure for cystic fibrosis might finally be in sight.

> Was Danny Bessette healthy 12 years ago?
> Who was Danny a symbol for?
> What does *in sight* mean in this context?

Danny, then a cherubic-faced four year old, was pictured on the cover of the journal Science the week it published a dramatic breakthrough:

> What does *then* refer to?
> Why is Danny described as cherubic-faced?
> Why did Danny's picture appear on the cover of a journal?
> How often is Science published? Does the reader need to know that?
> What expectation is established by the phrase *dramatic break-through*? How might a *dramatic breakthrough* contrast with a *breakthrough*?

Scientists had found the gene that, when defective, causes the debilitating and ultimately fatal disease.

> What gene did scientists find?
> Is finding this gene a *breakthrough*?
> Finding implies hunting. Where would scientists hunt for the gene?
> Do genes cause diseases?

The discovery, one of the first of its kind, inspired giddy optimism in researchers and affected families alike.

> If *kind* means a type of discovery, then what type of discovery is being invoked?
> What are the *affected families* affected by?
> Why might the researchers and the families feel giddy optimism and not just optimism?

2. **What background information does the reader need to read the following text, and what inferences must be drawn?**

> Flat Branch, N.W.—Amid the rolling green hills of North Carolina's central plateau, on the edge of hog farm country, there's a strong whiff of prosperity in the air.
>
> Embraced by politicians and business leaders as an alternative to tobacco and all its uncertainties, large factory-style hog farms—some housing 10,000 or more animals—have brought jobs and wealth to depressed rural communities....
>
> (*The Washington Post*, August, 17, 2001, p. 1)

Analyzing Text
Lily Wong Fillmore

By analyzing features of language in the texts students are reading, teachers can draw their students' attention to aspects of text that might present difficulty—words, phrases, structures, and so forth. Let's take a look at the following aspects of academic English in a typical expository text—*Volcanoes*, one of the texts used in the video.

Vocabulary—the multiple meanings and uses of words; choice of words reflecting subtle gradations of meaning for effect; choice of words for precision.

Grammatical structures—the means for organizing sentences and foregrounding or backgrounding ideas.

Cohesive devices—the grammatical means for linking ideas into larger, coherent discourse.

Rhetorical devices—the grammatical means for structuring texts into effective discourse.

Phraseological patterning—the natural, idiomatic, or preferred ways of expressing ideas in the language, without which text could be grammatical but nonetheless not natural—the elusive stuff of really knowing a language.

Volcanoes that erupt regularly are known as *Active Volcanoes*. There are about six hundred active volcanoes on the Earth's surface. However, only fifty to sixty active volcanoes erupt in any given year. (Caption: Cotopaxi volcano in Ecuador.)

Whether sitting in silence or erupting with violence, volcanoes have intrigued people for thousands of years. In an attempt to explain the immense power and unpredictable behavior of volcanoes, our ancient ancestors created myths about evil gods that lived within volcanoes. When angered, the gods would display their fury with eruptions.

Today, scientists explain volcanoes without relying on angry gods. However, the true causes for *Volcanic Eruptions* are as fascinating as the ancient myths. (Caption: Heimaey volcano in Iceland.)

From *Volcanoes*, by Michael George © 1993 by Creative Education. Reproduced with permission. (Pages 10-11)

Want to try your hand at identifying features of the language used in this text to talk about with students?

Vocabulary

1. This text includes terms used that are associated with the topic of the book and the broader area of knowledge surrounding it—in this case, volcanoes and earth science or geology. Calling attention to these words, linking them together in a memorable way, will help students associate them with a background knowledge structure or *schema*. Some of these are technical terms; some are not. Can you find words and phrases (both technical and non-technical) that are associated with a volcano schema? Which words are associated with earth sciences or geology?

2. Words have to be considered in context, so we should look at the phrases in which words are used. There are some interesting phrases in this excerpt: *sitting in silence or erupting with violence*, etc. How might one call attention to such phrases, and how can students be given opportunities to try their hand at using such phrases?

Grammatical Structures and Devices

1. In texts like this one, a lot of information tends to be packed into a sentence; and while the sentences are not particularly long, they are quite compressed. In order to show how they are structured and how structure affects meaning, we might want to unpack some of these sentences with students. For example, consider this sentence:

   "In an attempt to explain the immense power and unpredictable behavior of volcanoes, our ancient ancestors created myths about evil gods that lived within volcanoes."

The teacher could help students unpack this sentence by asking them leading questions:

Q: Who was attempting to explain?
A: (Ancient ancestors)

Q: What does "ancient ancestors" mean?
A: (People related to us who lived a long time ago.)

Q: What were these people attempting to explain?
A: (The immense power and unpredictable behavior of volcanoes.)

Q: Why were they attempting to explain it?
A: (Because they didn't understand.)

Q: What does "unpredictable behavior" mean?
A: (Behavior that people can't predict. They don't know when it's going to happen.)

Q: So how did the ancient ancestors explain the power and unpredictable behavior of the volcanoes?
A: (They created myths—made up stories.)

Q: What were the myths about?
A: (Evil gods)

Q: What does this sentence tell you about the evil gods?
A: (They live inside volcanoes.)

The result of unpacking the sentence might look like this:

> People in ancient times (you might think of them as our ancient ancestors) didn't understand how volcanoes behaved or how they could be so powerful. They knew that volcanoes were powerful, but they didn't know where their power came from. They couldn't predict what volcanoes would do. They tried to explain volcanoes by inventing stories about them. They created myths about gods. The gods in these myths were evil. These evil gods lived inside volcanoes.

Take another sentence and unpack it in a similar fashion. How would you help students put the pieces back together again? Why would doing that be valuable to them?

2. There are several relative clauses in this text. Relative clauses provide explicit information about someone or something. For example, in "Volcanoes **that erupt regularly**" and "evil gods **that lived within volcanoes**," the bold part beginning with the relative pronoun is the relative clause. It provides explicit information about the previous noun phrase. Other relative pronouns are *who, whom, which, whose X, when,* and *where.* These are the so-called WH-question words. It might look as if *that* is different—but is it? Which WH-Q word might it correspond to? Consider how you might draw students' attention to the ways these words are used:

> Some volcanoes are called active volcanoes. What volcanoes? Volcanoes that erupt regularly.

> Our ancient ancestors created myths about evil gods. What evil gods? Evil gods that lived in volcanoes.

Invent another sentence on the topic of volcanoes and figure out how you would help students understand its structure.

Cohesive Devices

1. Notice that the writer uses various devices to move from general information about active volcanoes, their number, and the annual incidence of eruptions, to how people have always been intrigued and awed by them, and then back to the present. Take a look at the

various devices used (vocabulary choice, the exploitation of structures, etc.) to make smooth transitions and to tie the whole thing together. What are some of those devices, and how might attention be called to them?

2. All three sentences in the second paragraph begin with a phrase that is not the subject of the sentence. Why might the author have made these structural choices? Think of it in terms of cohesion. How might students be helped to see why the writer said it the way he did?

Rhetorical Devices

1. Notice that the author refers to "our ancient ancestors created myths" instead of saying something like "ancient myths told about...." What's the writer doing here? How did we get into the picture, and what is he trying to get us to do here? What other rhetorical devices is the writer using to pull us into this text?

2. There are two sentences in this passage that begin with the word *however*. Why *however*? How is it used, and what does it mean?

Phraseological Patterning

1. There are numerous interesting phrases that are not exactly clichés but are nonetheless familiar in academic texts like this one. For example, *"in any given year," "in an attempt to explain," "ancient myths,"* etc. Can you find some other sentences, phrases, and so on that are familiar sounding?

2. Phraseological patterning is a really hard-to-define concept—not at all easy to specify—and yet we can tell when it is violated. Consider this little excerpt from a student's essay reported by Scarcella (personal communication, March, 1994). The assignment was for students to write about a time they might have done something on a dare that they later regretted.

1   On Thanksgiving day in 1991, one event that I took a dare changed my life forever. Two

2   years ago, the relationship between my stepmother and I were so bad that we don't even

3   talk to each other for a while. I don't remember exactly how our argument started. At the

4   time, I was seventeen, and I was also young, unmature, and impulsive. We both angry.

5   We both used ugly and bad words yelled at each other. By the time that I could

6   remember, we both walked toward the garage door. It was at there, one event, one

7   moment, one action that I took for a dare taught me a lesson later on I will remember for

8   the rest of my life. **While all the anguish were inside my heart like lava that has been**

9   **waited inside the volcano that needed to be explore badly.** Before I could really

10   remember with conscience, I had use my hand and slaped on my stepmother's face.

11   Moments later she called 911. The police came and question me. I so scared and was

12   crying. The police told me if I do it again that they might put me in a jail next time. It was

13   a dare that I took for expressing the anguish that was inside my heart. The police scared

14   me badly that I made sure this situation will never occur in my life. I learned that no

15   matter how angry I was, I should never used my force make harm on others. I learned

16   that I have control my temper when it enter to the stage which I couldn't control. It is

17   better not to get mad when one is in fight. One really got mad, the best one can do is yell,

18   but never harming other people. In the end, while my life is still going on, I will never

19   take the dare that I did for as long as I live.

How might you have used the volcano text to help this young woman back when she was in the fourth grade (she had been in English-only programs for at least 8 years before she wrote this essay) learn how to talk about erupting volcanoes and molten lava at the smoldering hearts of volcanoes?

Supplementary Materials

D. Video Transcript

This transcript of the videotape is provided to help viewers locate sections of tape.

Narration: To be successful at school and later on in life, all students must become proficient readers. And all teachers must play a role in helping their students learn to read well.

But learning to read is complicated.

At regional conferences on Improving America's Schools, Professors Catherine Snow and Lily Wong Fillmore demonstrated some of the challenges that students face as they learn to read words and texts. Their presentations to professional developers and teachers emphasized that educators need to know a great deal about language and literacy so that they can support students' reading development.

Snow: Teaching children to read and, for that matter, teaching second language learners English is a very hard task, and it's a hard task for teachers precisely because those of us who teach and research in domains like language and literacy are the people for whom reading and language are relatively easy. Fish are the last creatures to discover water. Those of us who are interested in language and literacy are the last people to really have a good understanding of what's so hard about it. It's not something we know automatically. We think of language as a mechanism for communication. It's something we work with and that we use. But in order to help other people learn it, you have to be able to step back and think about where the problems arise. And that's true for language and it's true for literacy.

Wong Fillmore: Now what we know is that there are really important shifts in texts that children read at the third grade and at the fourth grade. And we will be looking at some of those texts and trying to figure out what kind of problems in those texts give problems to readers, and secondly, how can teachers make use of those texts as vehicles for helping children continue their development of English language skills and also increase their command of English literacy.

Reading Words

Narration: One way to understand the challenges that linguistically and culturally diverse students face in learning to read is to experience that difficulty first hand.

Snow: Now, as I said, it's very hard for those of us who are fluent, skilled, highly practiced readers to remember what it's like to struggle with beginning literacy. So in order to try to help us think about this, and help myself think about this, I should say, a couple of years ago, I decided that what I had to do was start to try to learn to read another language, put myself more or less in the position of a language minority child entering kindergarten or first grade. So I started studying Arabic.

Snow: This is just a random page from a newspaper and I'm sure you can tell from looking at the picture what it's all about. In fact, why don't we listen to the tape, and hear the first ... the first piece of the tape, which is the headline. So just read along, just do finger pointing here. Listen and point. (Arabic tape plays)

Snow: Now you were particularly disabled in that finger point reading exercise if you don't know that Arabic starts on this side and goes that way. Or if you happened to forget that. But it does. Arabic, like Hebrew and other Semitic languages, goes from right to left. And Arabic is what is referred to as a shallow orthography. Unlike English, a letter sort of makes a sound, and it makes that sound pretty much all the time. You don't have to worry about morphology and other complexities in the spelling system. However, one of the difficulties of reading Arabic is first of all that the letters change shape as a function of where they are in the word. We'll look at that in a minute. And secondly, that short vowels are not represented in the spelling. There are three long vowels, A, E, and O, and they are represented with letters in the spelling. But the short vowels a, e, o, are not. Okay, so you just have to know those. You have to sort of know how the word is pronounced.

Snow: There are 28 consonants. We're just going to concentrate today on five letters. That's kaaf, laam, miim, nuun and qaaf.

Okay? So these in fact, interestingly, in the Arabic alphabet, there's this little chunk in the middle that exactly corresponds—to which the English alphabet exactly corresponds, K, L, M, and N. Kaaf, laam, miim, nuun. And what we have here is just what the letter looks like in isolation and then what it looks like at the beginning, in the middle, and at the end of a word. So the little—that's Ku—it's not a word, it's just to show you how it looks. That's kaaf, at the beginning, kaaf in the middle, and then kaaf at the end. And that's laam, at the beginning, middle, and end, okay?

Snow: The first word there is *kanna*, means, *I was.* The second word is *kees*, means *bag.* *Sakeen, knife. Shuka, fork, semec, fish,* and *shubak, window.*

Snow: Now we're going to go on to laam. *Ling, lira, los, loge,* in the middle, *kilo,* the end, *neel, Nile River,* and *kuol.*

Snow: The N, the nuun, *neel, neer, nuor.* Tennis. *Kangar,* which means *kangaroo. Bint, min,* and *forn.* Okay? Four letters, three vowels, you know them now. Right? So this should be easy. Now, here comes the hard part. The sound, that qaaf, that K sound actually in English the K represents two quite distinct sounds. Right? The sound if you say *kill* or say *kiss,* to yourself, *kiss,* and sort of feel where you do the /k/, and now say *cool* to yourself and feel where you do the /k/. Right? Feel the *kiss,* the /k/ is sort of up in the front a little bit and the *cool,* it's way in the back. Well, that distinction is actually phonemic in Arabic. So in Arabic there's a distinction between *kiss* and *qiss* and *cool* and *qool.* I'm not producing it perfectly, but certainly any Arabic or native Arabic speaker can hear it, and those two sounds are represented by two different letters. And the /k/, the back one, is represented by this last letter we're going to do here, which is qaaf, not kaaf, but qaaf. So this is *qam, qul, qarnan, raqaqat,* and *noqinaq.* Sorry, sorry, sorry. *Naqineq.* That means sausages. *Naqineq.* And *waraq.*

Snow: And we have a text here. An Arabic text. There's a translation underneath, to give you semantic context. All you need to do is just go through and write above the line, write N for the nuun, write L for the laam, write M for the miim.

Snow: And I mean, I realize this is not necessarily—this isn't perhaps the way you'd be teaching kids, but on the other hand, I hope it does help you understand this is just so much spaghetti unless you've had certain experiences which a lot of kids have not had. Right? When I entered my Arabic class, I literally couldn't tell these letters apart, just as the sort of experience you're having now. And why is that? Well, because I didn't—I hadn't spent the first, the previous four years of my life having people point out signs in Arabic to me on shops and write my name for me and I didn't have Arabic refrigerator letters. I was in the same situation as many children entering kindergarten or first grade are, without a lot of emergent literacy or environmental print experience. Like you, I had to—I had a lot of trouble. I still have a lot of trouble hearing phonemic distinctions that are represented, that are straightforward and transparent for native Arabic speakers and that are represented in the Arabic writing system. But that's not too different from the situation of many children in our schools who are trying to spell the difference between *bat* and *vat*, but don't actually hear that distinction or the difference between *bin* and *bean* without being able to hear that distinction reliably.

Snow: Now we've got some words we can read. And that's the list of words in your handout; here they are. These are all easy words. I picked out words that I thought would make some sense. And this is one of the problems of course. When you're reading a language you don't speak, you could read the word correctly and you don't necessarily know whether you've read the word correctly. But these are words we should know, most of them. The first one is? It's, well, it starts with a … laam. Very good. And it goes—that's an E, the two dots underneath. It's *leemon. Lemon. Leemon.* Okay, the next one is—starts with a K. It starts *Ko a la. Koala.* Of course. Right? Now the next one is *ba loon.* Okay? Now, you don't know the B, but by this time, a little context can help. The next one here, *Amrika.*

Snow: So, I mean part of the reason for selecting these words is while I'm a deep proponent of the alphabetic principle and the fact that I think we need to teach kids letters and sounds and how they relate, that doesn't mean I think it makes no difference whether the letters and the sounds turn into words that make sense. And that's one of the big issues in thinking about literacy education for language minority children. How to focus enough direct instruction on a code, and on some rules for using the code, while not forgetting about the fact that meaning is what makes it all work. And if you're reading words, correctly or incorrectly, you have no way of knowing unless the words are words that are in your vocabulary and words that make sense to you.

Snow: Enough Arabic. You've, I hope, reached a point of frustration which helps you understand something about what kids go through.

Reading Text

Narration: Being able to read words is important, but it doesn't lead automatically to comprehending text. Next you'll see students reading texts that are appropriate for their grade levels. Some of the students are native speakers of English; others are not. The difficulties they encounter as they read show how challenging reading text can be.

Icebergs and Glaciers

Interviewer: What was this page about?

Teresa: About a thing that gets thick, and the thicker it goes, the thicker—the faster it goes.

Markus: The thicker. That it's faster and it's heavier on land, and ... that's it.

Interviewer: That's it? And what's the "it" that you're talking about?

Markus: The thicker.

Snow: I mean, part of what we tried to do here was we tried to get kids who could read the words. And it's clear that they could read the words. They read the words. But they didn't understand the text. The challenge is in putting the words together. So these are kids who've gotten far beyond in English they've gotten far beyond where we are in Arabic. Right? But that doesn't mean that the problems are solved. And that's sort of the point here.

Snow: And in fact if you look at the text, it's not such a crazy guess if you don't know what thicker means, right? The thicker. It starts out "The thicker." Now, so it's not crazy, but on the other hand, it does represent lack of understanding of the word *thicker* and lack of familiarity with this particular syntactic structure. Not something I would have predicted a fourth grader, even a second language speaker, would have trouble with.

Audience: One thing that I've noticed, and especially in science, the word *glacier* in Spanish and in English are cognates, 100%. Yet a child will not make that transfer into cognates and why that confusion if it is a 100% cognate.

Snow: Well, this is a very cogent observation, that *glacier* is a cognate. Many of these words that you encounter in science texts or in more complex texts are cognates. And yet children don't automatically make those connections. We presume that they're using background knowledge from Spanish. They, in fact, in fact they might not know these words in Spanish. And very often the words that one would learn in Spanish by having learned to read in Spanish, and having engaged in lots of reading in Spanish, are precisely the words that they don't know in Spanish either. So, what we might presuppose about transfer isn't always available. But even if children are very good speakers of Spanish, with very large vocabularies, they do need help to have it pointed out to them that they need to make those—that they could use the information. And in fact real intervention efforts to instruct children about the value of cross language transfer have been demonstrated to be important.

Wong Fillmore: Which also suggests that in situations where you can teach bilingually, that the same kind of support is needed in native language reading, and we cannot assume that children who speak the language natively necessarily have all the knowledge that is necessary to interpret the texts.

Rocks and Crystals

Interviewer: Now they said that the earth was like a perfectly boiled egg. Can you explain how the earth is like a perfectly boiled egg?

Emily: Like the inside is the core. And the outside is just like dirt and everything, and they have—if you dig there's rocks underneath it.

Interviewer: And how is that like a perfectly boiled egg?

Emily: I'm not sure.

Patricia: (silence)

Interviewer: Too weird an image? Yeah, a lot of people just read that and go, "What?!" Okay, so you mentioned the core. Did you learn what the core of the earth is made of?

Patricia: Yolk. Yolk.

Interviewer: Yolk.

Joe: The crust of the earth, the crust of the earth is just like the shell of the egg: thin and hard. And the mantle in the earth is just like ... I don't know what that white stuff is called ... in between it.

Interviewer: Okay. The white stuff.

Joe: Yeah, the white stuff would probably be, well, is getting closer to the core. You'd be getting closer to the core. And right in the middle of the core would be the yolk in the egg, which would be the exact center, which is the base of all of it.

Snow: So here we have a text which uses a metaphor that the earth is like an egg, to help children understand. Emily was working hard and yet I don't get the sense that Emily was making—was helped at all by the metaphor. Right? I mean, she sort of has this sense of the layers, but whether this egg metaphor helped her is quite unclear.

Snow: I take it that the author's goal here was to invoke an egg in which the white is hard and the yolk is liquid. And that key issue, that the core of the earth is molten metal and liquid, was something that even Joe didn't actually express. Right? That he didn't actually get that. So you're absolutely right. It wasn't—it was a very remote set of relationships to invoke.

Snow: So, Patricia, when asked what is the center of the earth, she said the yolk, and as we see the text invoked that kind of mistake, and said yolk, or core. And we don't know whether she's never encountered the word *yolk* before and thus doesn't know that it actually refers to egg and not to earth, or whether she was actually doing a good job of utilizing the metaphor. And these are the kinds of observations that, I mean, it's a tiny little piece of text here, right? It's a couple of questions from each of these children. And yet it's a little bit of a window onto how hard these texts are in ways that we might not have foreseen.

Caterpillars

Georgiana: It was about a Mourning Cloak Caterpillar. It was about what the Mourning Cloak Caterpillar eats, what it looks like, and where you could find it.

Interviewer: Why do you think this caterpillar is called a "mourning cloak" caterpillar?

Norida: Cause it wakes up in the morning.

Georgiana: Because the color of their skin is like the color of one of those old-fashioned funeral clothes that women wore.

Interviewer: And, tell me, do you know what *mourning* means?

Georgiana: Well, I know the definition of the homophone to it, but not really.

Interviewer: But not this *mourning*. Okay. Could you guess?

Georgiana: It's a type of cloth?

Snow: Gina says, "Do you know what mourning means?" She says, "Well, I know the definition of the homophone to it." So she's given this very good definition of—description of why it's called the Mourning Cloak Caterpillar, which if you look at the text, is straight out of the text. It uses words like *funeral*. Does not connect, is not able to connect this to the word *mourning*. And then recognizes it's not a word she knows and Gina says, "Well, make a guess." And she says, "I think it's a kind of cloth." Okay? So, strong inferencing, not a lot of knowledge. There's a lot of stuff that kids like this have to have been taught in order to understand this text. And there's no way you can expect them to pick it up just from having vague exposure.

The Language of Texts

Narrator: Reading words and comprehending texts can be difficult for any student. The fact that school texts are written in academic English, which is subtly different from the kind of English we use in social interaction, adds another dimension to the challenge of literacy.

Wong Fillmore: Now let's take a look at academic English and consider what it is and what it isn't. It is standard English. It is standard English. But not all instances of standard English are academic English, all right? Academic English is often written, but not every instance of written English is academic English. It's used in school, but not every instance of language used in school is representative of academic English. It is often cognitively demanding, abstract, and context independent, but not always.

Wong Fillmore: The vocabulary is distinctive and tends to be more precise, but there's a whole lot more to it than just vocabulary.

Wong Fillmore: It is learned in school but just being in school where it is used does not guarantee that students will learn it and that's really important too. Something special has to happen in order for students to learn how to deal with it and to become users of it.

Wong Fillmore: The question is what kind of help will children need in order to learn this kind of English. I will argue that the best, most reliable way to help children acquire academic English is through literacy. And what it will take is for teachers to be calling attention, calling the student's attention to how language works in the texts that they are having the children read or that they are reading to children. Now children who have been exposed to a rich language experience in the home, whether or not it is based on written language, enter school with a real head start in literacy. But the question is how are students who do not know standard English, let alone academic English, going to learn to read and write successfully.

Wong Fillmore: And they need to be providing children with many, many, many literacy experiences at school, where— which focus not only on learning how to read and write, but rather on the language as well. All right now, what kind of help do LEP students need and how do teachers provide it? The secret is this: No matter what subjects teachers are teaching, no matter what materials they are covering, they must give some attention to language every single day and on each and every subject which is being taught. Now this constant attention to language has got to be based on the most reliable source of academic English, as I said before, which are well written texts.

Audience: If you ask science teachers to understand what the English teachers know about, I mean, and even as an English teacher I don't have the linguistic knowledge that either of you have. And if you're asking a science teacher to be able to anticipate all of that, then we're all going to have to go to school for a lot longer and we're all going to have to get paid a lot better to pay for our education.

Snow: That's the bottom line right there. That is in fact precisely what I would recommend. We all need to go to school a lot longer and if that means we have to get paid more, all right. Then the society would have to absorb those costs. But the fact of the matter is that it does take knowing more than the average undergraduate teacher education program can offer to do a good job of this. And so I think you're exactly right, that we do need to go to school longer.

Audience: Or get an English teacher and a science teacher together, you know. Let them help each other.

Wong Fillmore: Getting a science teacher and an English teacher together would just be incredible if they are willing to do that. Unfortunately, in many, many of the content teaching areas, people tend to think of themselves as specialists in their field, without considering how crucial a part language plays in what they're doing just as for an English teacher. So we've got to break down the kind of mindsets because kids have got to learn this kind of language.

Narrator: The language that's used in texts has special features that can make books difficult to comprehend. By analyzing the texts that their students read, teachers can help students understand difficult passages.

Interviewer: Tell about what you learned about from those two pages.

Lesley: Volcano erupts. And there are thousand of ... volcanoes. And they erupt silently. And thousand of people have ... have....

Carina: That volcanoes ... that the volcanoes ... the scientists discovered that the evil gods, when they got mad....

Interviewer: Can you tell me?

Carina: They were ... the volcanoes erupt.

Interviewer: Why do you think they say that thousands of years ago our ancient ancestors thought that there were evil gods in the volcano? Why do you think they thought that?

Lesley: Because it was, it was too hot and it was red.

Carina: Because maybe they did.

Wong Fillmore: As you could tell from the transcripts and from these little segments, the kids really did not understand this text. They were able to pull little phrases from them, put them together in some attempt to come up with answers. But the problem here is that these children are not unusual. They are not poor readers necessarily. But they really did not understand this text. Now you read through the text. You saw what it was like. And I would guess that all of you here understood the text perfectly well. Why? Because you knew this information already. And it was just a reminder. It just triggered what you already knew about volcanoes and how they erupt and people's beliefs about volcanoes. But let's think a little bit about what you saw in this text material. What made it difficult?

Audience: I think, it has been my experience that I see this phenomenon in texts that are supposedly simplified for either special education youngsters or second language learners. And what it does, it's almost like a summary of what another major piece would have been and so you miss the transitions and it's very confusing and makes it more difficult for the children.

Wong Fillmore: That is really an important observation. You get this kind of confusing text especially when materials are written down for language learners. And so the idea is that you want to keep the sentences short. You want to keep the text short. You want to somehow make active, you know, "whether sitting in silence or erupting with violence." Okay, the idea is to make a text simple for language learners or for students who are not so—deemed to be so able to read a long text. That many, many things are left out and what you end up with is a kind of summary, which makes it ten times harder to read than a longer text, a much longer text with the pieces filled in. And that's a real problem. It's giving the most difficult kinds of texts that assume the greatest amount of knowledge and background to the kids who presumably are going to have difficulty reading. We cannot assume that short equals easy.

Wong Fillmore: What's interesting here, by the way, is that texts like this come at about the fourth grade, when rather than having a science text book with a great many pictures, with activities and so forth, at about the fourth grade, social studies, science texts, and the like begin to carry a kind of meaning payload. You read those texts to get information, the assumption being that by the fourth grade children know how to read well enough to be able to extract information from texts and to be able to understand those materials. Presumably by fourth grade, children—even children who begin with no English—will understand English well enough to be able to wrestle with a text like this. But as we can see from these children reading the texts, it wasn't so.

Wong Fillmore: And it's really important to think about not just teaching isolated vocabulary items but rather in any text on any subject you are going to find that there are little clusters of words that go together in a particular schema. And you'll find lots of words like that in this particular text. Calling attention to such words, talking about what they mean, talking about how they relate to the larger subject is one way that you can make them memorable for the kids so that the next time they hear the word *lava* up will come all of the other words they will have learned from this particular text, all right. And so the words that are related to the volcano or the geology schema are a natural in this text. Also in this text there are some really interesting descriptive contrasts that are made with adjectives and adjectival phrases such as "strange pasty material," "relatively thin," and so forth. And so drawing the students' attention to those, talking about what that means is another part of it. You saw the kids kind of reaching around in this text. They would pull together "thousands of people," but there wasn't anything about thousands of people here. They were putting things together in some attempt to make things memorable for themselves. Well calling attention to the ones that are used would be one way of doing that. Words have to be considered in context in the context that they are used so that some of these really interesting phrases used in this particular text the sitting in silence erupting in violence, etc., etc., calling attention to how they're used and giving kids opportunities to try their hands at using them in their own work. There are tons of grammatical devices and structures in this text. Catherine pointed out some of them to you, but consider some of these sentences and figure out how you might unpack something like "in an attempt to explain the immense power and unpredictable behavior of volcanoes, our ancient ancestors created myths about evil gods that lived within volcanoes." There are a lot of ideas packed into that. Work with your kids in unpacking that. All you have to do is say okay what is this saying and take out all of the little pieces. In the handout I unpack that for you. Putting it back together again gives the kids the opportunity to try to use some of these constructions that are a very important part of academic writing.

Narrator: Helping students develop the strong literacy skills they need to succeed at school calls for deep professional knowledge about language and reading, as well as expert teaching.

Audience: Our children today are just not reading enough material to also develop phraseologies that are in academic texts. And we need to instill the love of reading in them so they'll read, read, read much more. And I think that's really a key. Developing the information but getting them to want to read and to be reading in school all day long, not just in little teeny segments.

Snow: That's a very important observation, that reading, creating opportunities and demands to spend time reading, practicing reading is part of reading instruction.

Snow: Really the message here is we think the teachers need much more help than in general they have been given in order to address this. And we hope that's what people will leave thinking about and trying to work on.

Supplementary Materials

E. Questions and Comments from the IAS Conferences

This section reports workshop discussion between the presenters and the participants, most of whom were teachers, administrators, and other school personnel. The discussion is keyed to the sections of the video: Reading Words, Reading Texts, and the Language of Texts. Participant questions extend the discussion to issues such as testing, the educational role of students' first language, textbook publishing, culture, curriculum, constructivist teaching, and the children of poverty. Interaction included in the video is not repeated here.

Read these questions and comments after viewing each section of the video. In what ways are the observations made at the IAS regional conferences relevant to your experience?

Reading Words

Participant: I just want to say that I became so frustrated [with Arabic] that I just gave up.

Snow: I can understand that. It is a very frustrating task. Part of what is frustrating about it is somehow you see other people in the room who understand it and you don't and that makes it even worse. Perhaps the other people who understand it have some basic background knowledge that you don't. I was in a class full of people who were married to Arabic speakers. It was agonizing. They would come in with their homework all done and checked. (laughter)

Participant: There are several teachers writing curriculum ... around the names of the kids in the class, and I was wondering if that ties in to what you are saying because the names are meaningful: [Teachers can teach] the letters, sounds, everything stemming from [kids'] names. Do you think that is a reasonable thing to do?

Snow: Some teachers develop early literacy curricula around the children's names and use those as a basis for starting to practice these phoneme-grapheme relationships. I think that is exactly the right idea ... particularly for non-English speaking children, where names are immediately meaningful. This is a direct access to meaning. I wanted to take my Arabic teacher aside and say, "Could we at least print our names and put little placards on our desk so that we have some immediate reference. If I couldn't remember what an F is I could at least have a reference with Frank's name card." But I was too intimidated to be able to do that. But for children with very limited English capacity, finding the words that they know (and that would often include the names of their classmates) as a way to get into teaching [sound-letter correspondence] is a wonderful specific idea. It doesn't get you an entire literacy curriculum, but it breaks the ice.

Participant: There was nothing for me to connect with [in the Arabic lesson]. It is all just print. I don't have any pictures, just this [newspaper]. That's it. That's not enough.

Snow: That's true. You might argue that children's books would help you, but that is part of the reason that I picked this picture and [headline]. It turns out that it doesn't really help that much. It gives you some target items to look for, but it doesn't really help you break the system. It just relieves the boredom a little bit. (laughter)

Participant: If you were able to listen to music or perhaps repeat some key phrases or do some TPR [Total Physical Response] so we could orally get used to it instead of starting out in a literate base, [that] might be helpful.

Snow: The comment was that it would have made a lot of sense to start out with an oral introduction of Arabic before people are given the print. I absolutely agree. I would argue that you would be better off ... particularly if you don't know how to read any language ... learning to listen to the language and speak the language for a couple of years before being asked to read it.... Well, we figured that you only signed up for a morning (laughter). But this is what we are doing to kids in kindergarten classrooms. We are taking kids who walk in the door that speak no English, starting to teach them the alphabet and letter sounds.... If it [i.e., reading Arabic] is hard for us, with all the literacy and meta-cognitive skills that we have, imagine what sense those kids are making of it. I agree entirely— thinking about sequencing oral language exposure and literate exposure to English is a very important thing to do for children who are being launched on their initial literacy instruction in English.

Participant: I think in this room we all have a frame of reference: We have some kind of reading ability and something to refer to if we are having a hard time.... But ... [thinking about] our [teaching] colleagues, many of the kids come with no references to reading and yet we are teaching them sound-letter [correspondence] and we expect [that to be enough to enable] them to read. My fear is that in most schools because of whatever restrictions you have ... your ESL curriculum, you are teaching the phonics, the letters, the sounds, [and] the next step is language arts. That distinction between ESL and language arts—you jump into language arts curriculum and that's like years ahead of them [ELLs] and they are expected to perform.

Snow: Often, what we do is focus—correct me if I misinterpret your comments—what we do is focus the ESL classroom on this kind of teaching of letter-sound relationships and then release children into regular classrooms where the language arts activities are making demands on their oral language skills that are not at all [those] for which the children are prepared. At the same time those are the kinds of language arts activities that these children need to participate in [in] order to become excellent speakers of English. This is getting us over to the topic of the next part. How do we think about doing a better job of this basic literacy instruction so that children are fluent and not terribly discouraged readers—and with any luck joyful readers at the word level, the level of simple text—and at the same time ... ensure that their oral language is being developed in ways that prepare them to participate in serious reading comprehension and serious discussion of the topics that come up in the classroom environment. That is the challenge. If they don't learn to read they won't learn the vocabulary that they will need for that participation. But if they are asked to participate in those discussions without the requisite language skills, they will also find it very discouraging.

Reading Text

Rocks and Crystals

Participant: The issue here is not necessarily a language issue, but a cultural issue. I submit that there are many monolingual [English] speakers who have no idea of what a boiled egg is, or at least what a perfectly boiled egg is.... We are not talking about second language acquisition. We are talking about the cultural involvement of content.

Snow: Complexity of the concept, a perfectly boiled egg, and the specificity of that concept is clearly something that isn't directly accessible even to the native English speakers here, which confirms your point.

Participant: It occurs to me that there is a logic to this and that the author has some gaps in his writing. Because yolk or core is a construct and truly the children grasp that the use of core implies a synonymous relationship. I would suggest the author has not taken into account both the experiences and potential level of instruction for a fourth grader.

Snow: It's hard to write this stuff [i.e., children's books], and people do a very bad job of it sometimes even with the best intentions. And furthermore, attempts to take complex content and turn it into a third grade reading level or second grade reading level or a fourth grade reading level often introduce these kinds of complexities in the service of trying to make the text simpler. So it's another whole issue about the people writing the ... books not knowing enough about language.

Participant: I'm not suggesting that this would make all of the difference in the world, but I wonder how deliberate it is that there is no picture attached to the text, no manipulatives. Obviously we are talking about an egg and slicing it in half and comparing a picture of the core of the earth. The connections ... [would be] more obvious for a child [if a picture appeared in the text].

Snow: There is a picture of the earth showing the layers but there isn't a picture of the egg.

Language of Texts

Volcanoes

Participant: I know you wanted to assume that their [i.e., the students'] inability to answer the question was because of the text. But I don't want to make that assumption. What I want to talk about is the kind of question that was asked—which in all cases, they were always descriptive questions. So let me talk about a performative question first. You would not ask a three year old, "How does a horse look like. What does a cow look like?" You would ask [for] performance.... You would say, "What does a cow do?" And the kid would say, "Moo, moo." So I think that with our children, they go through those Piaget type stages. And I think that descriptive kinds of questions are harder for them to answer. So I think maybe more appropriate would have been another kind of question like, "Do you think that that's right? Is the earth like an egg or is it more like a watermelon? Or is it more like an ice cream?" You know, in other words you'd ask a comparative question which would be the kind of question they could answer. I'm thinking they may have gotten something out of the text, but ... descriptive questions are not the kind of question they can deal with at that level.

Wong Fillmore: The question here—the comment has to do with the type of questions that the interviewer was asking, that these may not have been appropriate questions given the age and the background of the students. And that if more appropriate questions had been asked, they would have revealed the [students] were understanding the text.

I wanted to comment ... on whether or not these children understood more than was revealed through the questioning. The fact remains that LEP students, after they get to a certain point, and that is usually at about the grade level these kids are, just go all the way down in their comprehension of texts. And my point here is not so much to show that the children—these particular children didn't understand or couldn't respond to the questions. It's a lot more complicated than most of us assume that it is.

Snow: I would very much reinforce that answer. I don't think Piaget is relevant to thinking about this, frankly. I'm not a maturationist when it comes to reading and language development. These are not skills that mature. These are skills that children learn from having exposure and instruction. And if they haven't had opportunities to learn how to deal with these texts, then they're not going to be able to display comprehension. [The question asked by the interviewer] is a very fair question: What did you just read? This is a question that we expect kids to be able to answer every single day in school. And not only do we expect them to be able to answer it, but so often we presuppose that they can answer it that we don't even bother to ask the question. We expect them to have learned the material in the text because we haven't explored the ways in which the texts are complex and thus barriers to comprehension for these kids. So I think that it's crucial for us to come to a better understanding of how texts are difficult and how kids thus need to be explicitly helped to deal with these texts.

Participant: Why is it assumed that reading has to be the first, initial vehicle for the provision of information or knowledge? In the initial stages reading should be an expansion of information attained.

Wong Fillmore: The point is that it is assumed that reading is a vehicle for providing information—that this ought to be a confirmation of information learned in other, more accessible ways like through a video tape.... [Nonetheless, we need texts that are well written and accessible to students.] You and I have a powerful role to play in publishing. It is in our choice and our understanding of what texts have got to do that drive the textbook industry. The textbook publishers write according to what they believe will sell. Before they go out with a textbook series they have these focus groups [of educators] in California, Texas, Illinois, Florida and New York. No textbook series, no company will survive if they don't have at least one of those states adopt a series.... We drive what happens. They [i.e., textbook publishers] write to readability formulae ... which determine by sentence length, word frequency, whether or not these materials are readable at a particular grade level.... The words are counted and averaged over sentences and you get a mean length of a sentence. The words themselves are broken into syllables and those are counted so you get mean lengths of words. And all of that is supposed to tell you how difficult a text is.

About Instruction

Participant: I work with older children than the students you are speaking [about] and I wonder especially if you were working with 4th graders and trying to call attention to rhetoric without using words like rhetoric, that might be too abstract. My understanding in the early grades is that you really need to be as concrete as you can—to keep them motivated, to keep them looking your way instead of out the window. You would really have to be careful of how you break the language down to not lose them. I understand the importance of what you are saying—that if they don't understand how the language is being used, they are not going to make meaning from it. But how to go about doing that without losing their attention? It would seem to me to be another class. I'm worried about it being too abstract

Wong Fillmore: But children can deal with abstractions, and in learning any language there are going to be parts of the language which are concrete, which are somehow easier to get at on your own. And then there are going to be parts of the language which are abstract and where you really need for someone to say, "Hey look at this, why do you think...?" This is calling children's attention—raising their meta-awareness abut the language, and decisions to use the language, and what something means if it is said this way. "Why would a [writer] choose to tell us these 'volcanoes are sitting in silence' and what does it mean, 'erupting with violence?' Why do you think the writer said that?" You engage in talk. Not everything comes through to everyone, but if you are doing it every single day, every single subject ... you set yourself a goal: "I'm going to talk about five things/bits of the language." Trust me, it begins to add up. If something is too abstract this week for Jose—two weeks later you are doing something similar— because we do seem to run through the same kinds of material once our attention is called to something we are going to be picking up on other instances of the same kinds of constructions and uses. Interestingly this adds up. Didn't get it this time, the second time, or the third time, but bam, got it the fourth time and that's the way this kind of thing works.

Participant: Another possible complication that my neighbor here and I were talking about—your choices of what to teach, because knowledge keeps expanding. We have to make choices about what is crucial. Okay, so in each class, in each subject area, you are not only teaching the subject area, but you are teaching the way the language works. You are slowing down how much material you cover over the year, which means that you have to make more decisions abut what you are going to cover. Yes I think that you are right and that it will pay off. Not only will they have a deeper understanding of what they read—and that will help them later on—but later on they will not have covered the breadth of material that students need to know today.

Wong Fillmore: I could imagine weaving in this kind of discussion into the discussion of the materials so that ... you are not drawing out five things and then spending ten minutes on each. You are doing as you go along. See this is a real problem. If you understand the materials really well, then you are not necessarily paying attention to how the language works. [For] children who know the language, who are native speakers of English, what they read does not necessarily translate over to productive use. So they sort of understand the material but they could not put into words.... It is only after attention is called to the way that language is used and to what effect that children begin to command that kind of language. They begin to put these constructions and words into their own print and speech, and gradually they become more competent at it.

Snow: The issue here is—we are not focused on what to do on Monday morning; we are focused here on what we need to know in order to know what to do on Monday morning, and that is our real message here. Lily and I are not 3rd grade or 6th grade teachers—and actually I would love to hear from those of you who are 2nd or 4th grade teachers as to what you think is reasonable as to explicit teaching about language. But my argument is this—having been thinking about literacy instruction and the principles underlying literacy instruction—that children need to have access to information about the alphabetic principle and meaning, and the way in which the alphabetic principle gives them access to meaning. Access to meaning means knowing an enormous amount about spoken language, and that is true for native English speakers as well as second language speakers. We think that in the first grade classroom we are teaching literacy by teaching the alphabetic principle and giving kids lots of opportunities to read simple text, to develop fluency in reading. And that is true. But on the other hand if we are not spending at least that much time also focusing on development of oral language skills and development of vocabulary and development of complex discourse skills, then we are leaving kids with second grade literacy and blocking them from being able to be in a position to use their print skills to go on and really process texts like this. So the focus has to be on a parallel one on reading and language.

More About Instruction

Participant: We need to shift the emphasis to students. "Covering the curriculum" implies the teacher as actor. The student needs to discover the curriculum. We need to be conscious of the language that we use in the profession.

Snow: Let me restate: Metaphors like "cover the curriculum" might indeed reflect an attitude toward teaching and learning that is inherently unproductive. It shouldn't be teachers covering curricula—it should be students discovering curricula. The key point which I agree with is that nobody has ever demonstrated that coverage correlates with accomplishment, and in fact depth of analysis on a smaller number of topics may well turn out to be a better strategy. The key that Lily and I would like to emphasize is that there are certain things that kids are going to take away. It is probably not the facts, not the details of the coverage in the curriculum: It's the skills—that really knowing about reading and writing, those are skills that multiply, are applicable, and will enable these kids to operate in a wider variety of curricular contexts. Now once again, we understand that there are tests out there that are focused on facts and which are focused on specific content areas and that we are operating in a new assessment environment which makes achieving some of these goals very hard. Nonetheless, thinking about what kids really need to know, the ones that are going to get to the university and the ones that are not going to go beyond high school, I think it is really clear that we need to think about language and literacy much more at the center of that.

Wong Fillmore: If you have children who are LEP to begin with, if you have kids with limited experience with academic discourse and materials that would give them a familiarity with such language walking into the classroom, then there has got to be, I'm sorry but there is a huge, huge role for educators to play here. It has become increasingly unpopular over the last 20 years to say that "I'm teaching and I'm going to go over these materials." Somehow this implies that it is not good instruction if it is teacher-centered in some sense. If there is only one person in that classroom who knows this stuff, then guess who is going to have to talk about it. You get [English] language learners learning from [English] language learners and what you can get there is not a very deep understanding of how [the English] language works. This is where we really need to think about how language works in any kind of instruction and any kind of text.

Participant: I guess I want to clarify before I make the wrong assumption about what you are saying. There has been an emphasis on getting the teacher off the center stage, getting the kids to talk more to each other. I think what I hear you say is that the teacher needs to do more. Is that what you are saying?

Wong Fillmore: What I am saying is that not every technique that works, works when you have students with special needs to learn the language. In many such situations where teachers are so apprehensive about talking to kids, leading a discussion, guiding children, giving them corrective feedback, what you get is learners learning English from learners, and the outcome is something really interesting: It's "learnerese." It is a form of the language that falls way short of the target. Why? Because the target that they have been aiming at is not a fully realized form of the language as spoken by the only person in the classroom [who is proficient in Standard English]. And we're talking about schools where 90% of the kids are LEP, where no one but the teacher is a reliable speaker of the language and can reveal the nature of the language. In those situations you have discussions, but they have got to be carefully guided by a teacher who is providing input modeling, corrective feedback, and all of the kinds of things that are absolutely necessary for anyone to learn the language.... Ideally you have a teacher who speaks the students' native language so that the teacher can take what the kids say in the native language and put it into English as a model for what they intended to say. These are language teaching and development techniques. It is when kids are left on their own with none of this supportive feedback or instructional support that you end up with funny versions of the language.

Participant: I'm hearing a couple of things here. We have had a stress on constructivist learning for LEP students. And yet a lot of the things that you're talking about seem to presuppose the teacher as the conveyer of the knowledge and I wonder if you could comment on that.

Snow: How do you resolve the dilemma of making language and literacy learning constructive for children and the role of the teacher which we are presenting here as crucial, central, the source of a lot of knowledge. First of all, let's think about the LEP students. We have 25 Spanish-speaking children in a classroom, where there is one native speaker of English—namely the teacher. That single native speaker of English has an enormous responsibility, because if he or she is the source of knowledge about English, and I would argue that—and I've heard Lily argue that—you can't just kind of let it happen under those circumstances. You have to plan it, structure it, organize it. You've got to use every millisecond of the day, you know, in the most efficient way possible, to be sure ... that there is enough access to English in classrooms like that. Now if you've got a classroom of one Spanish speaker and 20 to 30 English-speaking kids, you can let it happen. Many kids think the classroom conversation in general will support English language literacy. That's not the situation for most of the LEP kids.

Participant: [My understanding] is that there are some principles in teaching and learning which work well enough where students already know the language of instruction. If they do not, then those same wonderful instructional strategies simply are ineffective and even worse, they can cause terrible problems. If you just turn those 25 non-English speakers loose so that they're interacting freely with one another, guess what's going to come out of it? If they speak the same language, there will be not very much English. If they speak different languages, they're going to use the only language they have in common, which is English, and ... since nobody knows the language very well, what you end up with is learnerese. It's a language which is not exactly English, and there are so....

Wong Fillmore: What these kids need is corrective feedback. They need useful, helpful, insistent corrective feedback from the get-go. So that, you know, they cannot assume that they don't have any problems with language.

Participant: We are focusing on language, not teaching necessarily. About 5 years ago there was a study in San Bernardino, the only one that I know of. One group of students were permitted to interpret what they read in their native language, and they were able to do that easily. Traditionally, we have insisted that they only interpret in English. What recommendations do you have for facilitating maximum level of interpretation? [What recommendations do you have for the use of the first language in acquiring English?]

Wong Fillmore: That kind of thing works very well if you have a bilingual teacher who understands what the kids are saying [and] can encourage them to think about the text and talk about it however they can. Ultimately, the need to develop English skills [means that] you have to get them to be able to talk about these topics in English as well. This does not mean that the kids ought to forget their native language, far from it. But there has got to be some encouragement for the kids to move increasingly towards greater and greater competence in the language they are learning as well as in the language they already know. And, by the way, just being able to speak a language does not mean that you can talk lucidly about it. I'm sure you all know English speakers who [can't] talk lucidly [about it]. You get practice in doing this, necessary practice.

Participant: We're talking about the reliance on the teacher. How do you address [the fact] that many of our teachers do not possess academic English in the content areas that they teach? As an administrator of bilingual education in my district, I'm constantly in the schools. As I pass by and walk through the halls and I hear what teachers are saying, [I see that] they are not models for students. What do we do?

Wong Fillmore: Same thing that we do with the children. There have to be teacher development opportunities ... for teachers to learn to talk about academic materials. If they are not getting it in the university training programs where they have been, then we provide [it] onsite.... It takes opportunities to talk about things at an abstract level. We need to relate to research, to materials out there, to big ideas. None of us was born talking that way.

Participant: All of this that you are presenting also applies to students from a generation of poverty. For all practical purposes they tend to be LEP students, but they have a social [language] register and we need to move them to the formal and the academic register. And so the training we need is how to present the material. Shame, shame, shame on any teacher that would use a textbook for instructional purposes for the academic content, but you use it for the language and how can the students learn about language to perform in the society. I come from a district with 60% poverty and we are talking about all kids.

Snow: These points are not just relevant to LEP students who are limited in English because they come from another language background, but also children whose English skills are limited because they come from families that have not provided them [with opportunities] to be read to ... [and] interesting conversations of the type that would help develop these skills. There is good descriptive data now [on] children entering first grade, normally developing children, perfectly healthy, competent, intelligent children from middle class families who enter first grade with vocabularies [of] 12 to 15,000 words. [In] families with much lower parental education, children can enter first grade with vocabularies of 3 to 5,000 words. The difference between knowing 3,000 words and 15,000 words of English translates into an enormous challenge for the first grade teacher. It means that we cannot let a minute pass by in first and second grade without thinking about vocabulary enrichment within the context of language enrichment. That is the task and it is as much a contribution to literacy as is teaching children about letters and sounds.

Participant: [I see] a contradiction or conundrum or both, meaning that the two points you raised earlier were you need to delay the introduction of written text until oral language is developed. But on the other hand, you need exposure, wide exposure to reading in order to develop the skills to understand academic language. How do you put those two together? Is it possible to introduce text simultaneously with oral language development?

Snow: Let me clarify that. I hope I didn't say to postpone the introduction of written text. I said postpone the introduction of formal reading instruction—the kind of exercise that you folks went through with the alphabet in Arabic. The best mechanism for helping young English language learners to develop oral language skills involves the use of written text— being read to, talking about books that are being read. But the point of this is to support language development, not to start to teach reading in the first year of exposure to oral English. Rich language, rich literacy environments—those are crucial. Formal reading instruction does not have to start at age five.

Supplementary Materials

F. Guidelines for Starting a Study Group

Study Groups

Study groups offer a democratic approach to professional development. They provide sustained opportunities for teachers to work together to explore issues and challenges that have direct impact on their professional lives and the lives of their students. They represent a radical shift from traditional professional development efforts. They require that teachers create and use knowledge, not merely receive it (Clair, 1998).

Suggested Guidelines for Study Groups that Focus on Literacy Instruction in Culturally Diverse Schools

- Groups include 6 to 12 members.
- Groups meet frequently (e.g., twice a month for two hours).
- Groups are open to all teachers. They include bilingual program, content area, and ESL teachers.
- Membership in the group is voluntary, but strong incentives are offered.
- Because study groups represent a radical shift from traditional professional development experiences, initial group meetings focus on developing group norms and discussing expectations.
- Leadership and accountability are shared, and sessions are interactive. All members are responsible for preparing for meetings, attending each one, contributing to activities, and taking turns facilitating the work.
- Group process is democratic. Group members are responsible for voicing concerns and proposing solutions.
- Group members build knowledge of educational linguistics (the role of language in teaching and learning), second language acquisition, assessing students' learning, diversifying instruction, and other topics of local interest by reading and discussing literature based in research and exploring its relevance to the local context. Outside professional development providers are contracted for work that the group members define.
- The group uses sustainable learning strategies that are tied to essential dimensions of literacy instruction. Productive strategies include, but are not limited to, examining student work, carefully observing classroom practice, and reading and discussing professional literature.

Supplementary Materials

G. Readings

ERIC/CLL

newsbulletin

ERIC CLEARINGHOUSE ON LANGUAGES AND LINGUISTICS   **CAL** CENTER FOR APPLIED LINGUISTICS   *Volume 23, No 1 Fall/Winter 1999*

Bilingual Children's Reading: An Overview of Recent Research

by Georgia Earnest García, University of Illinois at Urbana-Champaign

The research base on bilingual children's reading is limited. Much of the research on bilingual children's reading acquisition comes from outside the United States. The overview of research presented here is based primarily on a literature review that was written for the third volume of the *Handbook of Reading Research* (García, in press) and covers the period from 1989 through 1997.

The aim of this article is to articulate needed areas of research. The first part focuses on bilingual children from preschool through Grade 2; the second part focuses on bilingual children in Grades 3 through 12. Topics warranting further investigation are noted throughout the discussion. The article concludes with a brief summary of the types of research that need to be conducted.

Reading Acquisition of Young Bilingual Children

Metalinguistic Awareness

Research has shown that bilingual children younger than age 6 tend to outperform monolingual children on isolated tasks of metalinguistic awareness related to reading (see García, Jiménez, & Pearson, 1998). For example, in a comparative study of Yugoslavian preschool and kindergarten children, Göncz and Kodzopeljic (1991) found that bilingual children were significantly better than monolingual children at explaining how words such as *mosquito* and *ox* differed in their length and referents. In another study, Galambos and Goldin-Meadows (1990) found that young Spanish-English bilinguals in El Salvador outperformed their monolingual Spanish counterparts on sentence grammaticality tests in Spanish. More recently, Bialystok (1997) reported that 4- and 5-year-old bilingual preschoolers in Canada (French-English and Mandarin-English speakers) outperformed monolingual English-speaking

preschoolers on a metalinguistic task specifically related to beginning reading. Bialystok interpreted the superior performance of the bilingual children and the fact that they performed the task equally well in both languages to mean that they not only had a heightened knowledge of symbolic representation as encoded in text, but that they were also able to transfer this knowledge from one language to the other. Why bilingual children's metalinguistic advantage seems to disappear after the age of 6 is not known, although it could be due to the predominant tendency to provide schooling to bilingual children in only one language at a time, effectively limiting their continued bilingual development.

Important Role of First Language Literacy

Findings from two longitudinal studies highlight the important role that first language literacy appears to play in bilingual students' academic development. The first study was conducted by Collier and Thomas (1989). They reported that non-English-speaking immigrant children did best in American schools when they arrived in the United States at age 8 or 9 with already developed literacy skills in their native language. Children who arrived at age 5 or 6 without native-language literacy skills, and older children who had native-language literacy skills but faced high content and cognitive demands in English, did not fare as well.

Ramírez, Yuen, and Ramey (1991) compared the English academic performance of low-income Spanish-speaking children in Grades 1–6 enrolled in three types of U.S. programs: early-exit transitional bilingual education, structured immersion, and late-exit transitional bilingual education. They reported that by the end of third grade, there was no significant difference in the standard-

ized English language and reading test performance of the students enrolled in the structured immersion and early-exit programs, even though students in the early-exit programs had received much less English instruction. When they examined the performance of students in the late-exit programs, they discovered that those students who had the greatest opportunity to develop their Spanish between kindergarten and sixth grade increased their standardized English language and reading test performance at a significantly higher rate than students in the other programs and in the normed sample from the standardized test. They estimated that if the projected growth rate were sustained, students who had received instruction in Spanish 40% of the time would eventually catch up with their English-speaking peers and perform at grade level in English.

Cross-Linguistic Transfer of Knowledge, Strategies, and Skills

An underlying assumption of bilingual education is that bilinguals can transfer specific knowledge and skills acquired while reading in one language to reading in a second language. Verhoeven (1994) reported that the Dutch reading performance of Turkish children enrolled in a submersion program in the Netherlands predicted their Turkish reading performance. Similarly, the Turkish reading performance of Turkish students enrolled in a transitional program predicted their Dutch reading performance. He con-

continued on page 2

4646 40TH STREET NW • WASHINGTON DC 20016 • (202) 362-0700 • (800) 276-9834 • WWW.CAL.ORG/ERICCLL continued from page 1

cluded that students had applied reading skills learned in one language to reading in the other language. One of the few groups of researchers to document the specific types of skills and knowledge that transfer is Durgunoglu, Nagy, and Hancin-Bhatt (1993). Their study of Spanish-speaking first graders in the United States showed that the children's Spanish phonological awareness and word recognition significantly predicted their English word recognition and psuedo-English word recognition, indicating cross-linguistic transfer. Children who had phonological awareness and Spanish word recognition skills performed better on the transfer tasks than those children who could read some Spanish words but who demonstrated low Spanish phonological awareness. The researchers questioned whether young bilingual children who do not have phonological awareness in their first language should be taught these skills in their first language or in their second language. The extent to which bilingual children need to be taught phonological or orthographic elements that are characteristic of their second language but not of their native language, and whether this type of instruction can accelerate the students' second language literacy development, are topics that need further investigation.

Optimal Level of Second Language Oral Proficiency

Another important issue is the level of oral second language proficiency needed for bilingual children to acquire optimum second language literacy skills. (For a discussion, see August & Hakuta, 1997.) Three sets of researchers (Durgunoglu et al., 1993; Geva, Wade-Woolley, & Shaney, 1993; Verhoeven, 1994) reported that variables related to beginning reading (e.g., word recognition and phonological awareness), not oral proficiency levels, were more powerful predictors of bilingual children's reading performance in either language. This finding could be due to the fact that there is wide variation in the reading performance of young children who have attained a relatively high oral proficiency level in either language, and as a result, first language literacy might be the deciding factor. The finding also implies that a key predictor

of young bilingual children's reading is their ability to transfer knowledge about reading from one language to another.

Early Reading Instruction for Bilingual Children

Unfortunately, the type of instructional research that has been conducted with young bilingual children does not help us understand the issues raised in the acquisition research, nor does it help us to understand the types of instructional approaches that could be most beneficial. Ramírez et al. (1991) reported that the type of instruction they observed in structured immersion, early-exit, and late-exit transitional bilingual education classrooms, regardless of the language of instruction, was strikingly similar: passive instruction that did not promote complex language development or higher order thinking skills.

A few researchers have questioned some of the cultural and linguistic assumptions that underlie U.S. early literacy instruction. For example, Valdés (1996) noted that Mexican parents were puzzled by U.S. teachers' emphasis on the alphabet, because in Mexico teachers emphasized syllables. Teale (1986) recommended that educators investigate how writing could be tapped as an emergent literacy activity. In a study of low-income homes, including Latino homes, he found little evidence of parent-child book reading, but considerable emphasis on writing.

A few evaluations of intergenerational literacy programs have been published. The results of these indicate that children's emergent literacy development seems to be enhanced when the emphasis is on the home language (Brown-Rodriguez & Mulhern, 1993). When instruction was provided in English only, the children seemed to improve their oral English but not their emergent literacy development (Thornburg, 1993).

A number of researchers found that bilingual children enrolled in predominantly English settings had difficulty participating in storybook reading when native language support or English as a second language (ESL) modifications were not available. Thornburg (1993) reported that bilingual children did not respond to English storybook reading when teachers used a cognitive approach emphasizing story grammar and predic-

tion questions. Battle (1993) described how a bilingual teacher effectively used native language support to structure daily storybook read alouds in English for her Mexican-American kindergartners by presenting summaries of the books in Spanish, translating parts of the books during the read-aloud, and allowing the children to participate in either language during group discussions.

Very few researchers have investigated the type of Spanish reading instruction offered to young bilingual children. *Reading Recovery* (Escamilla, Andrade, Basurto, & Ruiz, 1990 & 1991) and *Success for All* (Calderón, Tinajero, & Hertz-Lazarowitz, 1992) have been tried with U.S. Spanish-speaking children, but the results still have not been widely evaluated or published. Although specialists in early childhood education warn against using group-administered, standardized achievement tests with young children, Goldenberg (1994) credited improvements in first- and second-graders' standardized reading test scores in Spanish to the inclusion of an academic code focus in kindergarten, a more balanced code-literature reading approach in first grade, and systematic efforts that involved the children's families in their early literacy development.

Reading Development of Older Bilingual Children

Reader and Textual Factors

Three sets of researchers have compared monolingual and bilingual students' reading comprehension in the majority language in terms of background knowledge, vocabulary difficulty, and use of metacognitive and cognitive strategies (Droop & Verhoeven, 1998; García, 1991; Jiménez, García, & Pearson, 1995, 1996). Looking across the studies, the results show that bilingual students in Grades 3, 5, 6, and 7 had less background knowledge and less familiarity with the vocabulary in majority language texts than monolingual students from the majority group. García (1991) reported that when differences in prior knowledge were controlled, there was no difference in the reading test performance of bilingual Latino and monolingual Anglo fifth and sixth graders, although the bilingual students still did worse on questions that required them

continued from page 2

to use background knowledge. Droop and Verhoeven (1998) reported that when third-grade Turkish students in the Netherlands read culturally appropriate texts that were linguistically simple, they outperformed their Dutch counterparts. However, when they read culturally appropriate texts that were linguistically complex, there was no significant difference in performance between the Turkish and Dutch students. The interplay among vocabulary knowledge, background knowledge, and textual complexity, and the circumstances that affect bilingual readers' effective use of background knowledge, are topics that merit further investigation.

A small number of researchers have compared the cognitive and metacognitve strategy use of bilingual Latino and monolingual Anglo students. The results seem to depend on how the students' strategy use was assessed, the ages of the students, and whether the students' performance was examined by reading level. Padrón, Knight, and Waxman (1986) reported that third- and fifth-grade bilingual Latino students used fewer and less sophisticated cognitive and metacognitive strategies in English than monolingual Anglo students. However, in a qualitative think-aloud study that focused on documenting the reading strategies of sixth- and seventh-grade bilingual Latino readers, Jiménez et al. (1996) reported that there was no substantial difference in the comprehension monitoring and meaning-making strategies demonstrated by the two groups of successful English readers: three monolingual Anglo readers and eight bilingual Latino readers. The students who demonstrated the fewest and the least sophisticated strategies were the three bilingual students who were not successful English readers.

Cross-Linguistic Transfer of Strategies

A number of researchers have studied the cross-linguistic transfer of knowledge and strategies in Spanish-speaking students' reading. Several researchers have investigated bilingual Latino students' use of Spanish-English cognates to figure out unknown English vocabulary. Although Nagy, García, Durgunoglu, and Hancin-Bhatt (1993) concluded that fourth-, fifth-, and sixth-

grade Latino students made use of cognates to figure out unknown English vocabulary, they also noted that the fourth graders identified fewer cognates than the older students, and all the students seemed to underutilize cognates.

Other researchers have compared the types of strategies that bilingual students use while reading in their two languages. Intermediate and high school bilingual Latino students reported using the same strategies while reading in the two languages, implying cross-linguistic transfer (Calero-Breckheimer & Goetz, 1993). In a qualitative think-aloud study of fourth-grade bilingual Latino students who were strong Spanish readers, García (1998) also reported that the students' reading profiles across the two languages were similar, implying cross-linguistic transfer. However, the students' actual use of strategies across languages varied according to text genre, text difficulty, and students' language dominance and reading ability. Because text genre made a difference in the type of strategies demonstrated, García recommended that researchers assess students' use of strategies across both expository and narrative text.

Not all bilingual readers have an intuitive sense of transfer or make use of cross-linguistic strategies. Jiménez et al.'s (1995, 1996) research with successful and less successful bilingual English readers revealed that the successful readers had a unitary view of reading across the two languages. They knew that knowledge and strategies acquired in one language could be used while reading in the other language. They also made occasional use of strategies unique to bilinguals, such as cognates, code-switching, and translating, to enhance their reading comprehension. However, this unitary view of reading, cross-linguistic transfer of knowledge and strategies, and use of bilingual strategies did not characterize the less successful bilingual readers, who thought that they had to keep their two languages separate or they would become confused. How characteristic the Jiménez et al. findings are for other bilingual readers and whether transfer instruction can help bilingual students

improve their reading needs to be investigated on a much wider scale.

The Role of Second Language Oral Proficiency

The research findings on the role of second language oral proficiency in older bilingual students' second language reading seemed to vary according to research design (quantitative or qualitative), the type of oral language proficiency measures employed, the ages of the students, and the students' success at reading. For example, in a quantitative study, Peregoy and Boyle (1991) reported a strong and significant relationship between third-grade Spanish-speaking students' English reading test performance and their English oral proficiency. In contrast, findings from a qualitative, think-aloud study of 12 fifth-grade Spanish-speaking students (Langer, Bartolomé, Vásquez, & Lucas, 1990) showed that the use of meaning-making strategies across the two languages was more predictive of the reading of the better readers than their English or Spanish oral proficiency. Students' instructional experiences typically were not taken into account in this type of research, although they probably should have been. Additional research needs to examine the different factors that appear to affect the relationship between second language oral proficiency and second language reading for older bilingual students.

Reading Instruction of Older Bilingual Students

Because bilingual children frequently attend poorly funded schools, they often receive poor quality reading instruction in both languages (Padrón, 1994; Ramírez et al., 1991). Unfortunately, very little is known about the type of reading instruction that optimally promotes older bilingual children's literacy development in their first or second language. Even less is known about the type of instruction that helps bilingual students transition from bilingual or ESL to all English instruction.

Several researchers have shown that immersing older bilingual children in second language literature-based activities, such as storybook reading or process writing, without taking into account their second language status, is not very effective (Elley, 1991; Reyes, 1991). On

continued from page 3

the other hand, Elley concluded that high quality ESL instruction along with literature-based activities did have a positive effect on 8- to 10-year-old South Pacific and Southeast Asian English language learners who were already literate in their first language.

Four sets of researchers developed or tested approaches with bilingual readers that were designed to improve their use of metacognitive and cognitive reading strategies. Although the data were limited, reciprocal teaching, question-answer relationships (QARs), and getting bilingual students to self-generate questions while reading appeared to be effective strategies (Muñiz-Swicegood, 1994; Padrón, 1992). In a qualitative study with five low-literacy seventh-grade Latino students, Jiménez (1997) reported that the students benefited from cognitive strategy lessons that used culturally familiar texts, emphasized reading fluency and word recognition skills, and taught the students how to resolve unknown vocabulary, ask questions, and make inferences, as well as use bilingual strategies such as searching for cognates, translating, and transferring knowledge from one language to the other.

Despite the huge problem that unknown English vocabulary poses for bilingual readers, very few researchers have attempted to address this problem. García (1996) reported that 10 out of 13 fourth-grade Mexican-American students were able to access cognates to figure out unknown English vocabulary after receiving individualized scaffolded instruction on cognate recognition. In an experiment with seventh- and eighth-grade bilingual students (predominantly Cambodian), Neuman and Koskinen (1992) concluded that viewing captioned television during a science program provided these students with the type of comprehensible input they needed to improve their acquisition of English reading vocabulary.

Further research needs to examine the effectiveness of culturally responsive approaches, such as Moll and Gonzalez's (1994) "cultural funds of knowledge approach," where teachers were trained as ethnographers and documented literacy activities in Latino homes and communities that they later incorporated into classroom literacy instruction.

A key component of this research was the positive shift in teacher attitudes toward working-class Latino students and their families.

Final Thoughts

It is clear that there is a need for more research on bilingual children's reading development and instruction. It would be interesting to know if bilingual children in the United States have a metalinguistic advantage over their monolingual counterparts. Given the presence of dual immersion programs, it seems possible for us to begin to study biliteracy development and the roles of first language literacy and second language oral proficiency. The transfer assumption that underlies bilingual education makes it imperative for more researchers to investigate the types of strategies, skills, and knowledge that bilingual readers transfer from reading in one language to the other, and whether instruction can help to facilitate such transfer.

We really know very little about the types of instruction that promote bilingual students' literacy development. We need longitudinal research that documents the types of instruction that bilingual students receive in and outside of bilingual programs, taking into account the languages and settings in which they are taught and the influence of social, political, and cultural factors. Research that evaluates packaged instructional programs (such as *Reading Recovery*), instructional approaches (such as balanced literacy, literature-based reading, or reader response) and instructional innovations (such as reciprocal teaching and cultural funds of knowledge) is also critical. Also needed is instructional research that addresses bilingual students' unique needs, such as second language vocabulary instruction and transfer instruction.

In undertaking this research agenda, it is important to employ a bilingual perspective, where we investigate and identify findings unique to bilinguals at the same time that we carefully evaluate the application of monolingual findings to bilingual populations (García, 1998). We also need funds and commitment that parallel the increasing presence of English language learners in the United States.

References

August, D., & Hakuta, K. (1997). *Improving schooling for language-minority children: A research agenda.* Washington, DC: National Academy Press.

Battle, J. (1993). Mexican-American bilingual kindergarten collaborations in meaning making. In D.J. Leu & C.K. Kinzer (Eds.), Examining central issues in literacy research, theory, and practice. *Yearbook of the National Reading Conference, 42,* 163-69.

Bialystok, E. (1997). Effects of bilingualism and biliteracy on children's emerging concepts of print. *Developmental Psychology, 33,* 429-40.

Brown-Rodríguez, F.V., & Mulhern, M.M. (1993). Fostering critical literacy through family literacy: A study of families in a Mexican-immigrant community. *Bilingual Research Journal, 17,* 1-16.

Calderón, M. E., Tinajero, J.V., & Hertz-Lazarowitz, R. (1992). Adapting cooperative integrated reading and composition (CIRC) to meet the needs of bilingual students. *Journal of Educational Issues of Language Minority Students, 10,* 79-106.

Calero-Breckheimer, A., & Goetz, E.T. (1993). Reading strategies of biliterate children for English and Spanish tests. *Reading Psychology, 14,* 177-204.

Collier, V.P., & Thomas, W.P. (1989). How quickly can immigrants become proficient in school English? *Journal of Educational Issues of Language Minority Students, 16,* 187-212.

Droop, M., & Verhoeven, L. (1998). Background knowledge, linguistic complexity, and second-language reading comprehension. *Journal of Literacy Research, 30,* 253-271.

Durgunoglu, A., Nagy, W.E., & Hancin-Bhatt, B.J. (1993). Cross-language transfer of phonological awareness. *Journal of Educational Psychology, 85,* 453-465.

Elley, W.B. (1991). Acquiring literacy in a second language: The effect of book-based programs. *Language Learning, 41,* 375-411.

Escamilla, K., Andrade, A., Basurto, A., Ruiz, O. (1990, 1991). *Descubriendo la lectura: An early intervention Spanish literacy project.* Annual Conference Journal. Washington, DC: National Association for Bilingual Education.

Galambos, S.J., & Goldin-Meadows, S. (1990). The effects of learning two languages on levels of metalinguistic awareness. *Cognition, 34,* 1-56.

García, G.E. (1991). Factors influencing the English reading test performance of Spanish-speaking Hispanic children. *Reading Research Quarterly, 26,* 371-92.

continued from page 4

García, G.E. (1996). *Improving the English reading of Mexican-American bilingual students through the use of cognate recognition strategies*. Paper presented at the National Reading Conference, Charleston, South Carolina.

García, G.E. (1998). Mexican-American bilingual students' metacognitive reading strategies: What's transferred, unique, problematic? *National Reading Conference Yearbook, 47*, 253-63.

García, G. E. (in press). Bilingual children's reading. In M. Kamil, P. Mosenthal, P.D. Pearson, & R. Barr (Eds.), *Handbook of reading research* (Vol 3). New York: Longman.

García, G.E., Jiménez, R.T., & Pearson, P.D. (1998). Metacognition, childhood bilingualism, and reading. In D.J. Hacker, J. Dunlosky, & A.C. Graesser (Eds.), *Metacognition in educational theory and practice* (pp. 193-219). Mahwah, NJ: Erlbaum.

Geva, E., Wade-Woolley, L., & Shaney, M.. (1993). The concurrent development of spelling and decoding in two different orthographies. *Journal of Reading Behavior, 25*, 383-406.

Goldenberg, C. (1994). Promoting early literacy development among Spanish-speaking children: Lessons from two studies. In E.H. Hiebert & B.M. Taylor (Eds.), *Getting reading right from the start* (pp. 171-99). Boston: Allyn and Bacon.

Göncz, L., Kodzopeljic, J. (1991). Exposure to two languages in the preschool period: Metalinguistic development and the acquisition of reading. *Journal of Multilingual and Multicultural Development, 12*, 137-63.

Jiménez, R.T. (1997). The strategic reading abilities and potential of five low-literacy Latina/o readers in the middle school. *Reading Research Quarterly, 32*, 224-43.

Jiménez, R.T., García, G.E., & Pearson, P.D. (1995). Three children, two languages, and strategic reading: Case studies in bilingual/monolingual reading. *American Educational Research Journal, 32*, 31-61.

Jiménez, R.T., García, G.E., & Pearson, P.D. (1996). The reading strategies of bilingual Latino/a students who are successful English readers: Opportunities and obstacles. *Reading Research Journal, 27*, 427-71.

Langer, J.A., Bartolomé, L., Vásquez, O., & Lucas, T. (1990). Meaning construction in school literacy tasks: A study of bilingual students. *American Educational Research Journal, 27*, 427-71.

Moll, L.C., & González, N. (1994). Critical issues: Lessons from research with language-minority children. *Journal of Reading Behavior: A Journal of Literacy, 26*, 439-56.

Muñiz-Swicegood, M. (1994). The effects of metacognitive reading strategy training on the reading performance and fluent reading analysis strategies of third grade bilingual students. *Bilingual Research Journal, 18*, 83-97.

Nagy, W.E., García, G.E., Durgunoglu, A., Hancin-Bhatt, B. (1993). Spanish-English bilingual children's use and recognition of cognates in English reading. *Journal of Reading Behavior, 25*, 241-59.

Neuman, S.B., & Koskinen, P. (1992). Captioned television as comprehensible input: Effects of incidental word learning from context for language minority students. *Reading Research Quarterly, 21*, 95-109.

Padrón, Y. (1992). The effect of strategy instruction on bilingual students' cognitive strategy use in reading. *Bilingual Research Journal, 16*, 35-52.

Padrón, Y. (1994). Comparing reading instruction in Hispanic/limited-English-proficient schools and other inner city schools. *Bilingual Research Journal, 18*, 49-66.

Padrón, Y., Knight, S.L., & Waxman, H.C. (1986). Analyzing bilingual and monolingual students' perceptions of their reading strategies. *The Reading Teacher, 39*, 430-33.

Peregoy, S.F., & Boyle, O.F. (1991). Second language oral proficiency characteristics of low, intermediate, and high second language readers. *Hispanic Journal of Behavioral Sciences, 13*, 35-47.

Ramírez, J.D., Yuen, S.D., Ramey, D.R. (1991).*Longitudinal study of structured English immersion strategy, early-exit, and late-exit transitional bilingual education programs for language minority children. Executive summary: Final report*. San Mateo, CA: Aguirre International.

Reyes, M. de la Luz (1991). A process approach to literacy using dialogue journals and literature logs with second language learners. *Research on the Teaching of English, 25*, 291-313.

Teale, W.H. (1986). Home background and young children's emergent literacy development. In W.H. Teale & E. Sulzby (Eds.), *Emergent literacy: Writing and reading* (pp.173-206). Norwood, NJ: Ablex.

Thornburg, D. (1993). Intergenerational literacy learning with bilingual families: A context for the analysis of social mediation of thought. *Journal of Reading Behavior, 25*, 321-52.

Valdés, G. (1996). *Con respeto: Bridging the distances between culturally diverse families and schools: An ethnographic portrait*. New York: Teachers College Press.

Verhoeven, L.T. (1994). Transfer in bilingual development: The linguistic interdependence hypothesis revisited. *Language Learning, 44*, 381-415.

eric/cll staff

Joy Peyton
Director

Jeanne Rennie
Associate Director

Kathleen Marcos
Asst Director for Technology

Craig Packard
User Services Coordinator

Laurel Winston
Acquisitions Coordinator

Lisa Biggs
Administrative Assistant

Sonia Kundert
Production Editor

Thom Raybold
Technology Specialist

The *ERIC/CLL News Bulletin* is published semiannually (Fall/Winter and Spring/Summer) by the ERIC Clearinghouse on Languages and Linguistics and is mailed free to U.S.-resident members of ACTFL and TESOL. Individual copies will be sent free on request. We regret that we cannot honor requests for multiple copies. This issue and past issues can be downloaded or printed from our web site at www.cal.org/ericcll/news/index.html. This newsletter is in the public domain and may be freely reproduced and disseminated without permission. Please address comments or questions to the *News Bulletin* editor:

Editor
ERIC/CLL News Bulletin
4646 40th Street NW
Washington DC 20016-1859

Phone 202-362-0700
Fax 202-363-7204
e-mail: eric@cal.org
www.cal.org/ericcll

This publication was prepared with funding from the U.S. Department of Education, Office of Educational Research and Improvement, National Library of Education, under contract no. ED-99-CO-0008. The opinions expressed herein do not necessarily reflect the positions or policies of ED, OERI, or NLE.

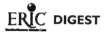 **DIGEST**

EDO-FL-01-02 • JUNE 2001

Lexical Approach to Second Language Teaching

OLGA MOUDRAIA, WALAILAK UNIVERSITY, THAILAND

The lexical approach to second language teaching has received interest in recent years as an alternative to grammar-based approaches. The lexical approach concentrates on developing learners' proficiency with lexis, or words and word combinations. It is based on the idea that an important part of language acquisition is the ability to comprehend and produce lexical phrases as unanalyzed wholes, or "chunks," and that these chunks become the raw data by which learners perceive patterns of language traditionally thought of as grammar (Lewis, 1993, p. 95). Instruction focuses on relatively fixed expressions that occur frequently in spoken language, such as, "I'm sorry," "I didn't mean to make you jump," or "That will never happen to me," rather than on originally created sentences (Lewis, 1997a, p. 212). This digest provides an overview of the methodological foundations underlying the lexical approach and the pedagogical implications suggested by them.

A New Role for Lexis

Michael Lewis (1993), who coined the term *lexical approach*, suggests the following:

- Lexis is the basis of language.
- Lexis is misunderstood in language teaching because of the assumption that grammar is the basis of language and that mastery of the grammatical system is a prerequisite for effective communication.
- The key principle of a lexical approach is that "language consists of grammaticalized lexis, not lexicalized grammar."
- One of the central organizing principles of any meaning-centered syllabus should be lexis.

Types of Lexical Units

The lexical approach makes a distinction between vocabulary—traditionally understood as a stock of individual words with fixed meanings—and lexis, which includes not only the single words but also the word combinations that we store in our mental lexicons. Lexical approach advocates argue that language consists of meaningful chunks that, when combined, produce continuous coherent text, and only a minority of spoken sentences are entirely novel creations.

The role of formulaic, many-word lexical units have been stressed in both first and second language acquisition research. (See Richards & Rodgers, 2001, for further discussion.) They have been referred to by many different labels, including "gambits" (Keller, 1979), "speech formulae" (Peters, 1983), "lexicalized stems" (Pawley & Syder, 1983), and "lexical phrases" (Nattinger & DeCarrico, 1992). The existence and importance of these lexical units has been discussed by a number of linguists. For example, Cowie (1988) argues that the existence of lexical units in a language such as English serves the needs of both native English speakers and English language learners, who are as predisposed to store and reuse them as they are to generate them from scratch. The widespread "fusion of such expressions, which appear to satisfy the individual's communicative needs at a given moment and are later reused, is one means by which the public stock of formulae and composites is continuously enriched" (p. 136).

Lewis (1997b) suggests the following taxonomy of lexical items:

- words (e.g., book, pen)
- polywords (e.g., by the way, upside down)
- collocations, or word partnerships (e.g., community service, absolutely convinced)
- institutionalized utterances (e.g., I'll get it; We'll see; That'll do; If I were you . . .; Would you like a cup of coffee?)
- sentence frames and heads (e.g., That is not as . . . as you think; The fact/suggestion/problem/danger was . . .) and even text frames (e.g., In this paper we explore . . .; Firstly . . .; Secondly . . .; Finally . . .)

Within the lexical approach, special attention is directed to collocations and expressions that include institutionalized utterances and sentence frames and heads. As Lewis maintains, "instead of words, we consciously try to think of collocations, and to present these in expressions. Rather than trying to break things into ever smaller pieces, there is a conscious effort to see things in larger, more holistic, ways" (1997a, p. 204).

Collocation is "the readily observable phenomenon whereby certain words co-occur in natural text with greater than random frequency" (Lewis, 1997a, p. 8). Furthermore, collocation is not determined by logic or frequency, but is arbitrary, decided only by linguistic convention. Some collocations are fully fixed, such as "to catch a cold," "rancid butter," and "drug addict," while others are more or less fixed and can be completed in a relatively small number of ways, as in the following examples:

- blood/close/distant/near(est) relative
- learn by doing/by heart/by observation/by rote/from experience
- badly/bitterly/deeply/seriously/severely hurt

Lexis in Language Teaching and Learning

In the lexical approach, lexis in its various types is thought to play a central role in language teaching and learning. Nattinger (1980, p. 341) suggests that teaching should be based on the idea that language production is the piecing together of ready-made units appropriate for a particular situation. Comprehension of such units is dependent on knowing the patterns to predict in different situations. Instruction, therefore, should center on these patterns and the ways they can be pieced together, along with the ways they vary and the situations in which they occur.

Activities used to develop learners' knowledge of lexical chains include the following:

ERIC CLEARINGHOUSE ON LANGUAGES AND LINGUISTICS • CENTER FOR APPLIED LINGUISTICS • 4646 40TH ST NW • WASHINGTON DC 20016-1859 • (202) 362-0700

- Intensive and extensive listening and reading in the target language.
- First and second language comparisons and translation—carried out chunk-for-chunk, rather than word-for-word—aimed at raising language awareness.
- Repetition and recycling of activities, such as summarizing a text orally one day and again a few days later to keep words and expressions that have been learned active.
- Guessing the meaning of vocabulary items from context.
- Noticing and recording language patterns and collocations.
- Working with dictionaries and other reference tools.
- Working with language corpuses created by the teacher for use in the classroom or accessible on the Internet (such as the British National Corpus [http://thetis.bl.uk/BNCbib/] or COBUILD Bank of English [http://titania.cobuild.collins.co.uk/]) to research word partnerships, preposition usage, style, and so on.

The Next Step: Putting Theory Into Practice

Advances in computer-based studies of language, such as corpus linguistics, have provided huge databases of language corpora, including the COBUILD Bank of English Corpus, the Cambridge International Corpus, and the British National Corpus. In particular, the COBUILD project at Birmingham University in England has examined patterns of phrase and clause sequences as they appear in various texts as well as in spoken language. It has aimed at producing an accurate description of the English language in order to form the basis for design of a lexical syllabus (Sinclair, 1987). Such a syllabus was perceived by COBUILD researchers as independent and unrelated to any existing language teaching methodology (Sinclair & Renouf, 1988). As a result, the Collins COBUILD English Course (Willis & Willis, 1989) was the most ambitious attempt to develop a syllabus based on lexical rather than grammatical principles.

Willis (1990) has attempted to provide a rationale and design for lexically based language teaching and suggests that a lexical syllabus should be matched with an instructional methodology that puts particular emphasis on language use. Such a syllabus specifies words, their meanings, and the common phrases in which they are used and identifies the most common words and patterns in their most natural environments. Thus, the lexical syllabus not only subsumes a structural syllabus, it also describes how the "structures" that make up the syllabus are used in natural language.

Despite references to the natural environments in which words occur, Sinclair's (1987) and Willis's (1990) lexical syllabi are word based. However, Lewis's (1993) lexical syllabus is specifically not word based, because it "explicitly recognizes word patterns for (relatively) de-lexical words, collocational power for (relatively) semantically powerful words, and longer multi-word items, particularly institutionalized sentences, as requiring different, and parallel pedagogical treatment" (Lewis, 1993, p. 109). In his own teaching design, Lewis proposes a model that comprises the steps, Observe–Hypothesize–Experiment, as opposed to the traditional Present–Practice–Produce paradigm. Unfortunately, Lewis does not lay out any instructional sequences exemplifying how he thinks this procedure might operate in actual language classrooms. For more on implementing the lexical approach, see Richards & Rodgers (2001).

Conclusion

Zimmerman (1997, p. 17) suggests that the work of Sinclair, Nattinger, DeCarrico, and Lewis represents a significant theoretical and pedagogical shift from the past. First, their claims have revived an interest in a central role for accurate language description. Second, they challenge a traditional view of word boundaries, emphasizing the language learner's need to perceive and use patterns of lexis and collocation. Most significant is the underlying claim that language production is not a syntactic rule-governed process but is instead the retrieval of larger phrasal units from memory.

Nevertheless, implementing a lexical approach in the classroom does not lead to radical methodological changes. Rather, it involves a change in the teacher's mindset. Most important, the language activities consistent with a lexical approach must be directed toward naturally occurring language and toward raising learners' awareness of the lexical nature of language.

References

Cowie, A. P. (Eds.). (1988). Stable and creative aspects of vocabulary use. In R. Carter & M. McCarthy (Eds.), *Vocabulary and language teaching* (pp. 126-137). Harlow: Longman.

Keller, E. (1979). Gambits: Conversational strategy signals. *Journal of Pragmatics, 3*, 219-237.

Lewis, M. (1993). *The lexical approach: The state of ELT and the way forward*. Hove, England: Language Teaching Publications.

Lewis, M. (1997a). *Implementing the lexical approach: Putting theory into practice*. Hove, England: Language Teaching Publications.

Lewis, M. (1997b). Pedagogical implications of the lexical approach. In J. Coady & T. Huckin (Eds.), *Second language vocabulary acquisition: A rationale for pedagogy* (pp. 255-270). Cambridge: Cambridge University Press.

Nattinger, J. (1980). A lexical phrase grammar for ESL. *TESOL Quarterly, 14*, 337-344.

Nattinger, J., & DeCarrico, J. (1992). *Lexical phrases and language teaching*. Oxford: Oxford University Press.

Pawley, A., & Syder, F. (1983). Two puzzles for linguistic theory: Native-like selection and native-like fluency. In J. Richards & R. Schmidt (Eds.), *Language and communication* (pp. 191-226). London: Longman.

Peters, A. (1983). *The units of language acquisition*. Cambridge: Cambridge University Press.

Richards, J., & Rodgers, T. S. (2001). *Approaches and methods in language teaching: A description and analysis* (2nd ed.). New York: Cambridge University Press.

Sinclair, J. M. (Ed.). (1987). *Looking up: An account of the COBUILD project in lexical computing*. London: Collins COBUILD.

Sinclair, J. M., & Renouf, A. (Eds.). (1988). A lexical syllabus for language learning. In R. Carter & M. McCarthy (Eds.), *Vocabulary and language teaching* (pp. 140-158). Harlow: Longman.

Willis, D. (1990). *The lexical syllabus: A new approach to language teaching*. London: Collins COBUILD.

Willis, J., & Willis, D. (1989). *Collins COBUILD English course*. London: Collins COBUILD.

Zimmerman, C. B. (1997). Historical trends in second language vocabulary instruction. In J. Coady & T. Huckin (Eds.), *Second language vocabulary acquisition: A rationale for pedagogy* (pp. 5-19). Cambridge: Cambridge University Press.

This digest was prepared with funding from the U.S. Dept. of Education, Office of Educational Research and Improvement, National Library of Education, under contract no. ED-99-CO-0008. The opinions expressed do not necessarily reflect the positions or policies of ED, OERI, or NLE.

ERIC CLEARINGHOUSE ON LANGUAGES AND LINGUISTICS • 800-276-9834 • ERIC@CAL.ORG • WWW.CAL.ORG/ERICCLL

ERIC Digests

ERIC Identifier: ED350885
Publication Date: 1992-12-00
Author:
Source: ERIC Clearinghouse on Languages and Linguistics Washington DC.

Myths and Misconceptions about Second Language Learning. ERIC Digest.

THIS DIGEST WAS CREATED BY ERIC, THE EDUCATIONAL RESOURCES INFORMATION CENTER. FOR MORE INFORMATION ABOUT ERIC, CONTACT ACCESS ERIC 1-800-LET-ERIC

This Digest is based on a report published by the National Center for Research on Cultural Diversity and Second Language Learning, University of California, Santa Cruz: "Myths and Misconceptions About Second Language Learning: What Every Teacher Needs to Unlearn," by Barry McLaughlin. Copies of the full report are available for $4.00 from Center for Applied Linguistics, NCRCDSLL, 1118 22nd St. NW, Washington, DC 20037

As the school-aged population changes, teachers all over the country are challenged with instructing more children with limited English skills. Thus, all teachers need to know something about how children learn a second language (L2). Intuitive assumptions are often mistaken, and children can be harmed if teachers have unrealistic expectations of the process of L2 learning and its relationship to the acquisition of other academic skills and knowledge.

As any adult who has tried to learn another language can verify, second language learning can be a frustrating experience. This is no less the case for children, although there is a widespread belief that children are facile second language learners. This digest discusses commonly held myths and misconceptions about children and second language learning and the implications for classroom teachers.

MYTH 1: CHILDREN LEARN SECOND LANGUAGES QUICKLY AND EASILY.

Typically, people who assert the superiority of child learners claim that children's brains are more flexible (e.g., Lenneberg, 1967). Current research challenges this biological imperative, arguing that different rates of L2 acquisition may reflect psychological and social factors that favor child learners (Newport, 1990). Research comparing children to adults has consistently demonstrated that adolescents and adults perform better than young children under controlled conditions (e.g., Snow & Hoefnagel-Hoehle, 1978). One exception is pronunciation, although even here some studies show better results for older learners.

Nonetheless, people continue to believe that children learn languages faster than adults. Is this superiority illusory? Let us consider the criteria of language proficiency for a child and an adult. A child does not have to learn as much as an adult to achieve communicative competence. A child's constructions are shorter and simpler, and vocabulary is smaller. Hence, although it appears that the child learns more quickly than the adult, research results typically indicate that adult and adolescent learners perform better.

Teachers should not expect miraculous results from children learning English as a second language (ESL) in the classroom. At the very least, they should anticipate that learning a second language is as difficult for a child as it is for an adult. It may be even more difficult, since young children do not have access to the memory techniques and other strategies that more experienced learners use in acquiring vocabulary and in learning grammatical rules.

Nor should it be assumed that children have fewer inhibitions than adults when they make mistakes in an L2. Children are more likely to be shy and embarrassed around peers than are adults. Children from some cultural backgrounds are extremely anxious when singled out to perform in a language they are in the process of learning. Teachers should not assume that, because children supposedly learn second languages quickly, such discomfort will readily pass.

MYTH 2: THE YOUNGER THE CHILD, THE MORE SKILLED IN ACQUIRING AN L2

Some researchers argue that the earlier children begin to learn a second language, the better (e.g., Krashen, Long, & Scarcella, 1979). However, research does not support this conclusion in school settings. For example, a study of British children learning French in a school context concluded that, after 5 years of exposure, older children were better L2 learners (Stern, Burstall, & Harley, 1975). Similar results have been found in other European studies (e.g., Florander & Jansen, 1968).

These findings may reflect the mode of language instruction used in Europe, where emphasis has traditionally been placed on formal grammatical analysis. Older children are more skilled in dealing with this approach and hence might do better. However, this argument does not explain findings from studies of French immersion programs in Canada, where little emphasis is placed on the formal aspects of grammar. On tests of French language proficiency, Canadian English-speaking children in late immersion programs (where the L2 is introduced in Grade 7 or 8) have performed as well or better than children who began immersion in kindergarten or Grade 1 (Genesee, 1987).

Pronunciation is one area where the younger-is-better assumption may have validity. Research (e.g., Oyama, 1976) has found that the earlier a learner begins a second language, the more native-like the accent he or she develops.

The research cited above does not suggest, however, that early exposure to an L2 is detrimental. An early start for "foreign" language learners, for example, makes a long sequence of instruction leading to potential communicative proficiency possible and enables children to view second language learning and related cultural insights as normal and integral. Nonetheless, ESL instruction in the United States is different from foreign language instruction. Language minority children in U.S. schools need to master English as quickly as possible while learning subject-matter content. This suggests that early exposure to English is called for. However, because L2 acquisition takes time, children continue to need the support of their first language, where this is possible, to avoid falling behind in content area learning.

Teachers should have realistic expectations of their ESL learners. Research suggests that older students will show quicker gains, though younger children may have an advantage in pronunciation. Certainly, beginning language instruction in Grade 1 gives children more exposure to the language than beginning in Grade 6, but exposure in itself does not predict language acquisition.

MYTH 3: THE MORE TIME STUDENTS SPEND IN A SECOND LANGUAGE

CONTEXT, THE QUICKER THEY LEARN THE LANGUAGE.

Many educators believe children from non-English-speaking backgrounds will learn English best through structured immersion, where they have ESL classes and content-based instruction in English. These programs provide more time on task in English than bilingual classes.

Research, however, indicates that this increased exposure to English does not necessarily speed the acquisition of English. Over the length of the program, children in bilingual classes, with exposure to the home language and to English, acquire English language skills equivalent to those acquired by children who have been in English-only programs (Cummins, 1981; Ramirez, Yuen, & Ramey, 1991). This would not be expected if time on task were the most important factor in language learning.

Researchers also caution against withdrawing home language support too soon and suggest that although oral communication skills in a second language may be acquired within 2 or 3 years, it may take 4 to 6 years to acquire the level of proficiency needed for understanding the language in its academic uses (Collier, 1989; Cummins, 1981).

Teachers should be aware that giving language minority children support in the home language is beneficial. The use of the home language in bilingual classrooms enables children to maintain grade-level school work, reinforces the bond between the home and the school, and allows them to participate more effectively in school activities. Furthermore, if the children acquire literacy skills in the first language, as adults they may be functionally bilingual, with an advantage in technical or professional careers.

MYTH 4: CHILDREN HAVE ACQUIRED AN L2 ONCE THEY CAN SPEAK IT.

Some teachers assume that children who can converse comfortably in English are in full control of the language. Yet for school-aged children, proficiency in face-to-face communication does not imply proficiency in the more complex academic language needed to engage in many classroom activities. Cummins (1980) cites evidence from a study of 1,210 immigrant children in Canada who required much longer (approximately 5 to 7 years) to master the disembedded cognitive language required for the regular English curriculum than to master oral communicative skills.

Educators need to be cautious in exiting children from programs where they have the support of their home language. If children who are not ready for the all-English classroom are mainstreamed, their academic success may be hindered. Teachers should realize that mainstreaming children on the basis of oral language assessment is inappropriate.

All teachers need to be aware that children who are learning in a second language may have language problems in reading and writing that are not apparent if their oral abilities are used to gauge their English proficiency. These problems in academic reading and writing at the middle and high school levels may stem from limitations in vocabulary and syntactic knowledge. Even children who are skilled orally can have such gaps.

MYTH 5: ALL CHILDREN LEARN AN L2 IN THE SAME WAY.

Most teachers would probably not admit that they think all children learn an L2 in the same way or at the same rate. Yet, this assumption seems to underlie a great deal of practice. Cultural anthropologists have shown that mainstream U.S. families and families from minority cultural backgrounds have different ways of talking (Heath, 1983). Mainstream children are accustomed to a deductive, analytic style of talking, whereas many culturally diverse children are accustomed to an inductive style. U.S. schools emphasize language functions and styles that predominate in mainstream families. Language is used to communicate meaning, convey information, control social behavior, and solve problems, and children are rewarded for clear and logical thinking. Children who use language in a different manner often experience frustration.

Social class also influences learning styles. In urban, literate, and technologically advanced societies, middle-class parents teach their children through language. Traditionally, most teaching in less technologically advanced, non-urbanized cultures is carried out nonverbally, through observation, supervised participation, and self-initiated repetition (Rogoff, 1990). There is none of the information testing through questions that characterizes the teaching-learning process in urban and suburban middle-class homes.

In addition, some children are more accustomed to learning from peers than from adults. Cared for and taught by older siblings or cousins, they learn to be quiet in the presence of adults and have little interaction with them. In school, they are likely to pay more attention to what their peers are doing than to what the teacher is saying.

Individual children also react to school and learn differently within groups. Some children are outgoing and sociable and learn the second language quickly. They do not worry about mistakes, but use limited resources to generate input from native speakers. Other children are shy and quiet. They learn by listening and watching. They say little, for fear of making a mistake. Nonetheless, research shows that both types of learners can be successful second language learners.

In a school environment, behaviors such as paying attention and persisting at tasks are valued. Because of cultural differences, some children may find the interpersonal setting of the school culture difficult. If the teacher is unaware of such cultural differences, their expectations and interactions with these children may be influenced.

Effective instruction for children from culturally diverse backgrounds requires varied instructional activities that consider the children's diversity of experience. Many important educational innovations in current practice have resulted from teachers adapting instruction for children from culturally diverse backgrounds. Teachers need to recognize that experiences in the home and home culture affect children's values, patterns of language use, and interpersonal style. Children are likely to be more responsive to a teacher who affirms the values of the home culture.

CONCLUSION

Research on second language learning has shown that many misconceptions exist about how children learn languages. Teachers need to be aware of these misconceptions and realize that quick and easy solutions are not appropriate for complex problems. Second language learning by school-aged children takes longer, is harder, and involves more effort than many teachers realize.

We should focus on the opportunity that cultural and linguistic diversity provides. Diverse children enrich our schools and our understanding of education in general. In fact, although the research of the National Center for Research on Cultural Diversity and Second Language Learning has been directed at children from culturally and linguistically diverse backgrounds, much of it applies equally well to mainstream students.

REFERENCES

Collier, V. (1989). How long: A synthesis of research on academic achievement in a second language. "TESOL Quarterly, 23," 509-531.

Cummins, J. (1980). The cross-lingual dimensions of language proficiency: Implications for bilingual education and the optimal age issue. "TESOL Quarterly, 14," 175-187.

Cummins, J. (1981). The role of primary language development in promoting educational success for language minority students. In "Schooling and language minority students: A theoretical framework." Los Angeles: California State University; Evaluation, Dissemination, and Assessment Center.

Florander, J., & Jansen, M. (1968). "Skolefors'g i engelsk 1959-1965." Copenhagen: Danish Institute of Education.

Genesee, F. (1987). "Learning through two languages: Studies of immersion and bilingual education." New York: Newbury House.

Heath, S. B. (1983). "Ways with words: Language, life, and work in communities and classrooms." New York: Cambridge.

Krashen, S., Long, M., & Scarcella, R. (1979). Age, rate, and eventual attainment in second language acquisition. "TESOL Quarterly, 13," 573-582.

Lenneberg, E. H. (1967). "The biological foundations of language." New York: Wiley.

Newport, E. (1990). Maturational constraints on language learning. "Cognitive Science, 14," 11-28.

Oyama, S. (1976). A sensitive period for the acquisition of nonnative phonological system. "Journal of Psycholinguistic Research, 5," 261-284.

Ramirez, J.D., Yuen, S.D., & Ramey, D.R. (1991). "Longitudinal study of structured English immersion strategy, early-exit and late-exit transitional bilingual education programs for language minority children. Final Report." "Volumes 1 & 2." San Mateo, CA: Aguirre International.

Rogoff, B. (1990). "Apprenticeship in thinking: Cognitive development in social context." New York: Oxford.

Snow, C. E., & Hoefnagel-Hoehle, M. (1978). The critical period for language acquisition: Evidence from second language learning. "Child Development, 49," 1114-1118.

Stern, H. H., Burstall, C., & Harley, B. (1975). "French from age eight or eleven?" Toronto: Ontario Institute for Studies in Education.

This report was prepared with funding from the Office of Educational Research and Improvement, U.S. Department of Education, under contract no. RI88062010. The opinions expressed do not necessarily reflect the positions or policies of OERI or ED.

ERIC® DIGEST

EDO-FL-00-08 NOVEMBER 2000

Teaching Educators About Language
Principles, Structures, and Challenges

NANCY CLAIR, CENTER FOR APPLIED LINGUISTICS

The promise of education reform is that all children will receive a quality education. But there are enormous challenges to reform, including resource inequities, an aging teaching force, and public doubts about school effectiveness. Moreover, school reform policies place enormous strain on teachers and students: Teachers need to implement new curricula and ensure that they are providing appropriate instruction. Students—including English language learners—must learn challenging content and pass statewide assessments in order to graduate in many states.

These new demands coincide with the well-documented changing face of the U.S. student population. More teachers are responsible for the education of children from diverse backgrounds—children who speak little or no English upon arrival at school, children who may have had interrupted schooling in their home country, and children whose families may have had little exposure to the norms of U.S. schools. In general, the U.S. teaching force is not well prepared to help culturally diverse children succeed academically and socially, because preservice teacher preparation programs have not offered sufficient opportunities for learning to teach culturally diverse students. As a result, many teachers have been learning on the job (Clair, 1995).

Fillmore and Snow (2000) assert that teachers need an understanding of educational linguistics—how language impacts teaching and learning—to do their work well. They argue that knowledge about language will enhance teachers' practice in general, and in particular, it will aid them in teaching literacy (Snow, Burns, & Griffin, 1998) and in working with English language learners (August & Hakuta, 1998). This Digest focuses on principles and structures for professional development of practicing teachers that can help them gain the knowledge they need about language and on some challenges to overcome for providing good professional development opportunities.

Language: A Central Component of Teachers' Work

Fillmore and Snow (2000) distinguish five teacher functions in which language is central. *Teachers are communicators*: They need to be able to communicate effectively and have strategies for understanding what students are saying. *Teachers are educators*: They are responsible for subject area instruction. They must also select educational materials and provide learning opportunities that promote second language acquisition for students who are learning English and that promote language development for native English speakers. They need to be able to distinguish language behavior that is developmentally predictable from that which is not and provide appropriate instructional intervention. *Teachers are evaluators* and their decisions have important consequences for students. There are far too many instances of students being placed in inappropriate educational programs because judgments of ability are influenced by misunderstandings of language behavior. *Teachers are educated people*: Information about language is essential to being a literate member of society. *Teachers are agents of socialization*. They play a central role in socializing children to the norms, beliefs, and communication patterns of school—and for immigrant children and native-born children from nonmajority backgrounds, to the patterns of mainstream U.S. culture. Basic knowledge about language and culture and how these systems can vary is fundamental to helping diverse students succeed in school.

Fillmore and Snow (2000) suggest that teachers should have knowledge of a number of topics regarding oral and written language, including the basic units of language, regular and irregular forms in English, vocabulary development, dialect regularity, academic English, language acquisition, the complexity of English spelling, patterns of rhetorical structure, quality and correctness in writing, and text comprehensibility. They suggest courses or course components that would allow teachers to learn essential information about language: language and linguistics, language and cultural diversity, sociolinguistics for educators in a linguistically diverse society, language development, second language teaching and learning, the language of academic discourse, and text analysis in educational settings.

Professional Development

What kinds of professional development experiences can help practicing teachers learn more about language and apply that knowledge to improving classroom practice? Clearly, short-term professional development experiences are inadequate: Teaching and learning are complex, and teachers need time to learn and experiment with new concepts in the classroom, just as their students do. Principles of effective teaching and learning for students extend to effective professional development for teachers (Rueda, 1998). To be successful, professional development must be long term, and it must incorporate opportunities for learning that center on teachers and students. Hawley and Valli (1999) suggest eight principles of effective professional development: It should be driven by an analysis of teachers' goals and student performance; it should involve teachers in the identification of what they need to learn; it should be school based; it should be organized around collaborative problem solving; it should be continuous and adequately supported; it should be information rich; it should include opportunities for the development of theoretical understanding; and it should be part of a comprehensive change process. Because in-service teacher education on language in teaching and learning must address teachers' attitudes toward language and toward students who speak languages other than English and dialects other than Standard English, it calls for extensive commitments of time. Teachers need time to reflect on the meaning of education in a pluralistic society, on the relationships between teachers and learners, and on social attitudes about language and culture that affect students (Clair, 1998; Gonzalez & Darling-Hammond, 1997).

There are a number of professional development structures that can incorporate these principles, including teacher networks and collaboratives (Renyi, 1996), university–school partnerships (Darling-Hammond, 1994), action research groups (Check, 1997), and teacher study groups (Clair, 1998). What these structures have in common are opportunities for teachers to learn together in coherent and sustained ways.

Challenges for Improving Professional Development

Designing opportunities for teachers to learn about language must link three essential elements: principles of effective professional development, appropriate content, and skilled professional developers. Integrating these elements presents significant challenges. First, understandings of effective professional development have changed much faster than practice. Many professional development experiences continue to be short term and disconnected from the reality of teachers' work. Second, under pressure to raise test scores, administrators and other educators may have trouble understanding how knowledge about language will help students succeed in school. Finally, identifying qualified professional developers with the knowledge, skills, and attitudes necessary to provide effective professional development on educational linguistics is daunting. These professionals need to have extensive knowledge about language and school reform and experience providing long-term professional development in schools. One way to overcome this challenge is teaming school personnel who provide professional development with university faculty or others with expertise in applied linguistics. Working together in schools, these teams can explore how language affects learning in particular contexts and build knowledge about language and education.

Conclusion

The demands of school reform and the changing face of the U.S. student population require that all teachers learn more about the role of language in teaching and learning. This knowledge can enhance their practice overall, improving their ability to teach literacy, and it can increase their effectiveness with students who speak languages other than English and dialects other than Standard English. Long-term professional development that views teacher and student learning as paramount must play a central role. The challenges are real but worth confronting, because high-quality education demands a well-educated teaching force.

References

August, D., & Hakuta, K. (Eds.) (1998). *Educating language minority children.* Washington, DC: National Academy Press.

Check, J. (1997). Teacher research as powerful professional development. *Harvard Education Letter, 13*(3), 6-8.

Clair, N. (1995). Mainstream teachers and ESL students. *TESOL Quarterly 29*, 189-196.

Clair, N. (1998). Teacher study groups: Persistent questions in a promising approach. *TESOL Quarterly 32*, 465-492.

Darling-Hammond, L. (1994). Developing professional development schools: Early lessons, challenge, and promise. In L. Darling-Hammond (Ed.), *Professional development schools: Schools for developing a profession* (pp. 1-27). New York: Teachers College Press.

Fillmore, L. W., & Snow, C. (2000). *What teachers need to know about language.* [On-line]. Available: http://www.cal.org/ericcll/teachers.pdf

Gonzalez, J. M., & Darling-Hammond, L. (1997). *New concepts for new challenges: Professional development for immigrant youth.* McHenry, IL, and Washington, DC: Delta Systems and Center for Applied Linguistics.

Hawley, W. D., & Valli, L. (1999). The essentials of effective professional development. In L. Darling-Hammond & G. Sykes (Eds.), *Teaching as the learning profession: Handbook of policy and practice* (pp. 127-150). San Francisco: Jossey-Bass.

Renyi, J. (1996). *Teachers take charge of their learning: Transforming professional development for student success.* New York: National Foundation for the Improvement of Education.

Rueda, R. (1998). *Standards for professional development: A sociocultural perspective* (Research Brief No. 2). Santa Cruz, CA: University of California, Center for Research on Education, Diversity & Excellence.

Snow, C. E., Burns, M. S., & Griffin, P. (Eds.). (1998). *Preventing reading difficulties in young children.* Washington, DC: National Academy Press.

This digest was prepared with funding from the U.S. Dept. of Education, Office of Educational Research and Improvement, National Library of Education, under contract no. ED-99-CO-0008. The opinions expressed do not necessarily reflect the positions or policies of ED, OERI, or NLE.

ERIC CLEARINGHOUSE ON LANGUAGES AND LINGUISTICS • 800-276-9834 • ERIC@CAL.ORG • WWW.CAL.ORG/ERICCLL

What Early Childhood Teachers Need to Know About Language

Considerable evidence exists that high-quality early childhood education programs for children from birth to age five can have long-lasting, positive consequences for children's success in school and later in life, especially for children from low-income families (Barnett, 1995; Frede, 1995). However, such programs are not available for all children who need them, nor are all programs of the quality that is necessary to achieve positive outcomes for children. In fact, only about 15% of child care centers are judged to be good or excellent. A recent study of a random sample of Head Start programs found that, while none of the programs was poor, the level of quality varied, and support for language and literacy learning was weak in many programs. Not surprisingly, children in the better quality programs out-performed children in lower quality programs on measures of learning and development (U.S. Department of Health and Human Services, 1998). Overall, Head Start children's expressive language skills were below national norms, but in the better quality programs, children's scores approached or matched those of their middle-class counterparts.

Recently, the U.S. Department of Education released a study of the skills and knowledge of a nationally representative cohort of children at entrance to kindergarten showing that social class and other group differences are already evident this early (West, Denton, & Germino-Hauskin, 2000). This finding suggests that kindergarten is too late to intervene in order to narrow the achievement gap. High-quality early childhood education programs have great potential for preventing later school failure, particularly if they place a strong emphasis on language development. For this reason, early childhood teachers need thorough knowledge about language and how to help children develop language and literacy skills. Often teachers haven't had opportunities to build the knowledge they need.

Early Childhood Education in Context

Early childhood programs operate in a variety of public and private settings under a range of state standards, all of which are minimal. Unlike the K-12 educational system, in which certified teachers with baccalaureate degrees are the norm, early childhood programs are often staffed by teachers with minimal qualifications.

The context of early childhood teacher preparation varies greatly depending on state licensing standards for teachers. It is only within the last decade that the majority of states have had specialized licensure for early childhood teachers (Ratcliff, Cruz, & McCarthy, 1999). A number of states have an early childhood license that begins at kindergarten, which means that there is no baccalaureate-level preparation specific to serving children ages birth through four. Many child care teachers attend associate-degree-granting institutions that offer majors in early childhood, but these programs do not provide the depth and breadth of language preparation that Fillmore and Snow (2000) call for in their article, "What Teachers Need to Know About Language."

The most significant barrier to ensuring that early childhood teachers have a broad and deep knowledge of language is the inferior compensation offered in most programs. Currently, teachers in programs for young children receive average salaries that are less than half of those of public school teachers (Cost, Quality, and Child Outcomes Team, 1995). This lack of adequate compensation leads to high staff turnover, making it impossible to recruit and retain well-qualified, well-educated teachers.

A further complicating factor for early childhood programs is that they are now being brought into the standards and accountability movement that has had a major impact on K-12 education. States are adding prekindergarten standards and assessments, and Head Start is incorporating child outcome data as part of its evaluation and accountability systems. Very young children, including children whose home language is not English, are expected to demonstrate specific progress on identified learning outcomes, which always include language and early literacy objectives.

Why Do Early Childhood Teachers Need to Know More About Language?

Fillmore and Snow identify five teacher roles that are relevant to working with young children: communicator, evaluator, educator, educated human being, and agent of socialization. Some of these roles are particularly critical for language learning because the early years are the foundation for what occurs later.

Communicator. The role of conversational partner is especially important in the preschool years when children are just beginning to acquire language. Young children develop their language skills through interactions with more accomplished speakers of the language, such as parents, family members, and teachers, as well as other children. When children are served in groups, the teacher's role as interlocutor is very complex. Often children whose language is more advanced are spoken to more often by adults. Thus children whose language development is lagging receive less language interaction than they need, and those who need less actually get more.

Although most early childhood teacher preparation programs address language development, little emphasis is given to the role of experience and learning, especially within the social and cultural context. Because this dimension of language acquisition is overlooked, many teachers do not know how to support children's language learning at various levels of development nor recognize when language development does not proceed as expected. Early childhood teachers need to talk with children in ways that ensure that their language continues to develop, their vocabulary increases, and their grammar becomes more complex.

Evaluator. More and more, early childhood teachers are thrust into the role of evaluators of children's language. This has always been a difficult role, because it involves attempting to identify children who may have developmental delays or disabilities. When young children are in the early stages of acquiring language, it is especially difficult to obtain valid and reliable data on their capabilities. Is performance variance attributable to normal, individual variation in rates of development, to experiential variation that is relatively easy to remediate, or to an actual delay? For teachers of students who speak a language other

ERIC CLEARINGHOUSE ON LANGUAGES AND LINGUISTICS • CENTER FOR APPLIED LINGUISTICS • 4646 40TH ST NW • WASHINGTON DC 20016-1859 • (202) 362-0700

96 *Part Three: Supplementary Materials*

than English at home or who speak a vernacular dialect of English, this role is even more complex.

Educator and educated human being. Teachers of young children need to be generalists in their knowledge of the world, because children are interested in just about everything that goes on around them. This does not mean that early childhood teachers must have every fact at their disposal, but it does mean that they need to have the extended vocabulary, curiosity, and skills to find out what they want to know.

Agent of socialization. By school entrance, the processes of socialization and language development are well under way. When children are served in programs outside of the home beginning as babies, toddlers, and preschoolers, socialization occurs simultaneously in two environments. It is especially important to respect students' home languages and cultures.

What Should the Early Childhood Classroom Teacher Know?

Although oral language development is a primary goal in early childhood programs, learning experiences and teaching strategies do not always support this goal. Layzer, Goodson, and Moss (1993) report on a study of the experiences of four-year-old children from low-income families in three types of preschool programs—Head Start, Chapter 1-funded prekindergartens, and child care centers. Acceptable levels of quality were maintained in all program types, and a wide variety of activities was generally available. However, some findings caused concern. For example, more than 25% of the classrooms did not have a story time, either for the whole group or for smaller groups. In addition, while teachers spent about two thirds of their time involved with children, only 10% of their time was spent in individual interaction. In fact, more than 30% of children across all classrooms had no individual interaction with a teacher. And in a study of language development at home, Hart and Risley (1995) found significant differences among social class groups in both quantity and quality of children's early language experience.

Early childhood teachers need to know the value of one-to-one, extended, cognitively challenging conversations and how to engage in such communication, even with reluctant talkers. They need to know how the lexicon is acquired and what instructional practices support vocabulary acquisition. They also need to know how to conduct story reading and other early literacy experiences that promote phonological awareness and prepare children for later success in reading (Snow, Burns, & Griffin, 1998).

Children also need time for social interaction and play with peers, which provide excellent opportunities for language acquisition. But here again, the potential of the early childhood context is unrealized. Opportunity for peer interaction may be insufficient because young children are perceived to need more instruction. Early childhood programs are often economically segregated so that children who need them most often lack peer models of school-sanctioned language. In addition, children who are acquiring English as a second language need to interact with native-speaker peers, but often they do not because they are served within their own language community and the teacher is the only one who speaks English.

Fillmore and Snow (2000) also address important issues pertaining to written language. One topic that they do not address in detail is phonics instruction and its relationship to precursors in phonological and phonemic awareness. Because phonics instruction has been so politically controversial, these are topics that childhood teachers need to know more about, including

appropriate ways for teaching young children. Most early childhood teachers do not have sufficient training in how to support early literacy learning. They need to know how much phonics children need to know, how to know which children need more or less explicit phonics instruction, and when to stop teaching phonics to which children.

Early childhood teachers should also have an understanding of cultural and linguistic diversity, and of learning and teaching that addresses the youngest age, including children who have not yet acquired a foundation in their home language.

Conclusion

Early childhood educators face tremendous challenges in supporting children's language development. Given that children acquire language best in meaningful contexts, through conversational interactions, and through encounters with written language, these must be the focus of instruction for teacher candidates.

Knowing what teachers need to know about language demands that the issue of teacher qualifications in early childhood education be addressed. Teachers of young children must obtain more education, better compensation, and greater respect. Their role in supporting children's language acquisition is the bare minimum of what they have to contribute to children's well-being and future potential.

References

Barnett, W.S. (1995). Long-term effects of early childhood programs on cognitive and school outcomes. *The Future of Children, 5,* 25-50.

Cost, Quality, and Child Outcomes Study Team. (1995). *Cost, quality, and child outcomes in child care centers* (Public Report, 2nd ed.). Denver: University of Colorado at Denver, Economics Department.

Fillmore, L. W., & Snow, C. E. (2000). *What teachers need to know about language.* [On-line]. Available: http://www.cal.org/ericcll/teachers.pdf

Frede, E. (1995). The role of program quality in producing early childhood program benefits. *The Future of Children, 5,* 115-32.

Hart, B., & Risley, T. (1995). *Meaningful differences in the everyday experience of young American children.* Baltimore: Brookes.

Layzer, J., Goodson, B., & Moss, M. (1993). *Life in preschool: Volume one of an observational study of early childhood programs for disadvantaged four-year-olds.* Cambridge, MA: Abt Associates.

Ratcliff, N., Cruz, J., & McCarthy, J. (1999). *Early childhood teacher education licensure patterns and curriculum guidelines: A state-by-state analysis.* Washington, DC: Council for Professional Recognition.

Snow, C., Burns, S., & Griffin, P. (1998). *Preventing reading difficulties in young children.* Washington, DC: National Academy Press.

U.S. Department of Health and Human Services. (1998). *Head Start program performance measures: Second progress report.* Washington, DC: Author.

West, J., Denton, K., & Germino-Hauskin, E. (2000). *America's kindergartners: Findings from the Early Childhood Longitudinal Study, kindergarten class of 1998-1999, fall 1998.* Washington, DC: U.S. Department of Education, National Center for Education Statistics.

This Digest is drawn from a commentary by Sue Bredekamp on "What Teachers Need to Know About Language," by Lily Wong Fillmore and Catherine Snow. Both that article and the commentary are available on the ERIC/CLL Web site (http://www.cal.org/ericcll).

This digest was prepared with funding from the U.S. Dept. of Education, Office of Educational Research and Improvement, National Library of Education, under contract no. ED-99-CO-0008. The opinions expressed do not necessarily reflect the positions or policies of ED, OERI, or NLE.

ERIC CLEARINGHOUSE ON LANGUAGES AND LINGUISTICS • 800-276-9834 • ERIC@CAL.ORG • WWW.CAL.ORG/ERICCLL

What Elementary Teachers Need to Know About Language

Over the past decade, education reforms have raised the educational bar that all children in the United States—including newcomers—must clear to finish school and participate in the economic and social world of the 21st century. These reforms place tremendous pressures on children and teachers: In addition to mastering the content-area curriculum, children must become skilled users of language. They must be highly competent in reading and writing to pass the various assessments that constitute gateways for completing school, getting into college, and finding jobs. Teachers need a wealth of content and pedagogical knowledge to ensure that they are providing appropriate instruction to all students. Teachers also need a thorough understanding of *educational linguistics*—how language figures in education. This foundation would support teachers' practice overall, and in particular, it would help them teach literacy skills (Snow, Burns, & Griffin, 1998), especially to English language learners (August & Hakuta, 1998). If approached coherently, preparation in educational linguistics would cover many items on lists of teacher competencies, such as skills in assessing children, individualizing instruction, and respecting diversity. This Digest summarizes some basic aspects of oral and written language about which elementary teachers need expertise in order to promote literacy. However, it is only one part of the formula for effective teaching. How literacy skills should be taught and how teachers can learn what they need to know about language are beyond the scope of this Digest.

What Should Classroom Teachers Know About Language?

Classroom teachers and other educators should be able to answer a basic set of questions regarding oral and written language. Underlying their knowledge should be an understanding that oral language proficiency developed first in the native language (and often in a second language) serves as the foundation for literacy and as the means for learning in school and out. Teachers need to know how written language contrasts with speech so they can help their students acquire literacy.

1. What are the basic units of language?

Teachers need to know that spoken language is composed of units, the smallest of which are sounds, called *phonemes* if they signal meaning differences (e.g., *bet* and *met* have different meanings because they start with different phonemes). Next come *morphemes*, sequences of sounds that form the smallest units of meaning in a language (*cat* is a morpheme of English and so is *–s*); *words*, consisting of one or more morphemes (*cats*); *phrases* (one or more words); and *sentences*. Crucial to an understanding of how language works is the notion of *arbitrariness*: Language units have no inherent meaning. A sequence of sounds that is meaningful in English may mean nothing at all in another language—or something quite

different. Understanding the variety of structures that different languages and dialects use to show meaning can help teachers see the logic behind the errors in their students' language use.

2. What is regular, and what isn't? How do forms relate to each other?

Proficient English speakers take for granted language irregularities that can be puzzling to younger and less fluent language users. An important part of acquiring a vocabulary suitable for academic contexts is knowing how to parse newly encountered words into their morphemes, rather than simply treating them as "long words." Teachers need to be aware of the principles of word formation in English since such knowledge can aid students in vocabulary acquisition.

3. How is the lexicon (vocabulary) acquired and structured?

Most classroom teachers recognize the need to teach vocabulary. Often, they identify and define technical or unusual words in texts. But knowing a word involves more than knowing its definition: It takes many encounters with a word in meaningful contexts for students to acquire it. It also requires understanding how the word relates to similar forms, how it can be used grammatically, and how it relates to other words and concepts. Effective vocabulary instruction requires that teachers understand how words are learned in non-instructional contexts through conversation and reading.

4. Are vernacular dialects different from "bad English" and if so, how?

To realize that differences among regional and social dialects of English or another language are a matter of regular, contrasting patterns in their sound systems, grammar, and lexicons—rather than errors—educators need a solid grounding in sociolinguistics and in language behavior across cultures. Schools must help children who speak vernacular varieties of English master the standard variety required for academic development, and they must respect the dialects that children use in their families and primary communities. Recognizing how language influences adults' perceptions of children and how adults relate to children through language is crucial to teachers' work. Educators need enough knowledge to keep speakers of vernacular dialects from being misdiagnosed and misplaced in school programs. In addition, they need knowledge about language variability in order to make sound decisions about instruction.

5. What is academic English?

Academic English is a cognitively demanding and relatively decontextualized register (Cummins, 1984). It relies on a broad knowledge of words, concepts, language structures, and interpretation strategies. Skills related to mastery of academic English include summarizing, analyzing, extracting and

ERIC CLEARINGHOUSE ON LANGUAGES AND LINGUISTICS • CENTER FOR APPLIED LINGUISTICS • 4646 40TH ST NW • WASHINGTON DC 20016-1859 • (202) 362-0700 interpreting meaning, evaluating evidence, composing, and editing.

Acquiring academic English is a challenge for both English language learners and native speakers. Few children arrive at school competent in this register. For the most part, academic English is learned over the course of schooling through frequent engagement in classroom talk, reading textbooks, and writing. Teachers need to recognize that all students need support to acquire the structures and vocabulary associated with academic English, and they need to know how to provide it.

6. Why has the acquisition of English by non-English speaking children not been more universally successful?

English language learners may be having a harder time learning English for academic success. Regardless of instructional program (e.g., bilingual, ESL, structured immersion), students who have entered school speaking little or no English may not be receiving the instruction they require to master academic English. Many teachers have been given misguided advice about what works for teaching English language learners—from letting children acquire the language naturally, to simplifying language use, to avoiding error correction. The message has been that direct instruction has no role. Fillmore (1991) found that children who are successful in acquiring English interact directly and frequently with people who know the language well. Such expert speakers not only provide access to the language, they also provide clues as to how to combine and communicate ideas, information, and intentions. Teachers must know enough about language and language learning to evaluate the appropriateness of various methods, materials, and approaches for helping students succeed.

7. Why is English spelling so complicated?

Unlike some other languages, English has not changed its spelling to eliminate inconsistencies and reflect changes occurring in its sound system over time. In addition, English generally retains the spelling of morphological units, even when the rules of pronunciation mean that phonemes within these morphological units vary (e.g., the second /k/ sound in *electric* and the /s/ sound in *electricity* have the same spelling). Errors in spelling can result from writers' inclination to write what they hear. English language learners' spelling errors may reflect limited exposure to written English forms, inadequate instruction, and transfer of general spelling strategies from another language. Understanding the complexities of English orthography can help teachers take sensible approaches to teaching it. Knowing how orthographies of different languages are organized also can help teachers figure out why spelling is more difficult for some students and why students make certain errors.

8. Why do students have trouble with narrative and expository writing?

All students need to learn the rhetorical structures associated with story telling and the various kinds of expository writing in English. However, many students bring to this task culturally based text structures that contrast with those expected at school. The emphasis in mainstream English stories is on getting the sequence of events correct and clear. This can seem so obviously correct to the monolingual speaker of English that the narrative of the Latino child, who emphasizes personal relationships more than plot, or that of the Japanese child, who may provide very terse stories, can be dismissed as incomprehensible (McCabe, 1995). Similarly with expository writing, argument structure varies across cultures. The topic sentences, paragraphs, and essays that are staples of English prose may be more difficult for students whose language experience includes other ways of expression.

9. How should the quality and correctness of a piece of writing be judged?

Teachers must have a solid-enough knowledge of grammar to support children's writing development and pinpoint problems in writing and interpreting text. Partly because teachers may feel insecure about their own writing, partly because students are not given opportunities to write frequently, and partly because teachers of writing are sometimes reluctant to correct students' writing, students may not be receiving the kind of corrective feedback that will help them be better writers. This problem is particularly acute for English language learners.

10. What makes a sentence or text difficult to understand?

Many educators erroneously associate simple sentences with ease in understanding and interpretation. For this reason, texts for English language learners are often composed of short, choppy sentences. The unintended result is that these simplified texts are far less readable than regular texts and may be insulting to readers. Moreover, because simplified texts are often unnatural, they cannot serve as exemplars of written academic English. With teachers' help, students can use well-written, grade-appropriate texts to learn content-area knowledge—as well as the vocabulary, grammatical structures, and rhetorical devices associated with academic writing.

Conclusion

As schools become increasingly diverse, education reforms will continue to put pressure on educators to provide appropriate instruction for all students. Teachers will continue to need access to a wide range of information to help students succeed, including information about the language that many of their students are learning. A thorough knowledge base in educational linguistics will support teachers' work overall and make school a place for students to succeed.

References

August, D., & Hakuta, K. (Eds.). (1998). *Educating language minority children*. Washington, DC: National Academy Press.

Cummins, J. (1984). *Bilingualism and special education: Issues in assessment and pedagogy*. Clevedon, England: Multilingual Matters.

Fillmore, L.W. (1991). Second language learning in children: A model of language learning in social context. In E. Bialystok (Ed.), *Language processing by bilingual children* (pp. 49-69). New York: Cambridge University Press.

McCabe, A. (1995). *Chameleon readers: Teaching children to appreciate all kinds of good stories*. New York: McGraw-Hill.

Snow, C.E., Burns, M.S., & Griffen, P. (Eds.). (1998). *Preventing reading difficulties in young children*. Washington, DC: National Academy Press.

This Digest summarizes a paper by Lily Wong Fillmore and Catherine Snow, "What Teachers Need to Know About Language," available at www.cal.org/ericcll.

This digest was prepared with funding from the U.S. Dept. of Education, Office of Educational Research and Improvement, National Library of Education, under contract no. ED-99-CO-0008. The opinions expressed do not necessarily reflect the positions or policies of ED, OERI, or NLE.

ERIC CLEARINGHOUSE ON LANGUAGES AND LINGUISTICS • 800-276-9834 • ERIC@CAL.ORG • WWW.CAL.ORG/ERICCLL

For Further Study

Anderson, V., & Roit, M. (1996). Linking reading comprehension instruction to language development for language minority students. *Elementary School Journal, 96*(3), 295-310.

Atwell, N. (1998). *In the middle: New understanding about writing, reading, and learning.* Portsmouth, NH: Boynton/Cook.

August, D., & Hakuta, K. (Eds.). (1998). *Educating language minority children.* Washington, DC: National Academy Press. (Chapter 3. Cognitive Aspects of School Learning: Literacy Development and Content Learning)

Baker, C. (1995). *A parents' and teachers' guide to bilingualism.* Philadelphia: Multilingual Matters.

Brisk, M. E., & Harrington, M. H. (2000). *Literacy and bilingualism: A handbook for all teachers.* Mahwah, NJ: Erlbaum.

Burns, M. S., Griffin, P., & Snow, C. E. (Eds.). (1999). *Starting out right: A guide to promoting children's reading success.* Washington, DC: National Academy Press.

Cummins, J. (1989). *Empowering minority students*. Sacramento, CA: California Association for Bilingual Education.

Fillmore, L., & Valadez, C. (1986). Teaching bilingual learners. In M. C. Wittrock (Ed.), *Handbook of research on teaching* (3rd ed., pp. 648-685). New York: Macmillan.

Fitzgerald, J. (1995). English-as-a-second-language learners' cognitive reading processes: A review of research in the United States. *Review of Educational Research 65,* 145-190.

Freeman, D. E., & Freeman, Y. (2000). *Teaching reading in multilingual classrooms*. Portsmouth, NH: Heinemann.

Gersten, R. (1996). Literacy instruction for language-minority students: The transition years. *The Elementary School Journal, 96*(3), 228-244.

Hakuta, K. (1986). *Mirror of language*. New York: Basic Books. (Chapter 6 contrasts adult and child second language acquisition.)

Murphy, C. U., & Lick, D. W. (2001). *Whole-faculty study groups*. Thousand Oaks, CA: Sage.

Neuman, S. B., & Roskos, K. A. (1993). *Language and literacy learning in the early years: An integrated approach*. Fort Worth, TX: Harcourt Brace.

Opitz, M. F. (Ed.). (1998). *Literacy instruction for culturally and linguistically diverse students: A collection of articles and commentaries*. Newark, DE: International Reading Association.

Samway, K. D., Whang, G., & Pippitt, M. (1995). *Buddy reading: Cross age tutoring in a multicultural school*. Portsmouth, NH: Heinemann.

Snow, C. E., Burns, M. S., & Griffin, P. (Eds.). (1998). *Preventing reading difficulties in young children*. Washington, DC: National Academy Press.

Internet Sites

Center for the Improvement of Early Reading Achievement
A collection of papers on early reading.
www.ciera.org

National Center for Family Literacy
Resources for family literacy services.
www.famlit.org

Center for Applied Linguistics (CAL)
Includes ERIC clearinghouses and research news and reports.
www.cal.org

National Association for Bilingual Education (NABE)
Association homepage focusing on the education of bilingual students.
www.nabe.org

National Clearinghouse for Bilingual Education (NCBE)
Provides a wealth of information, including full-text documents, about
the education of English language learners.
www.ncbe.gwu.edu

National Center for ESL Literacy Education (NCLE)

Focuses on ESL literacy issues for adults and out-of-school youth.
www.cal.org/ncle

Office of Bilingual Education and Minority Language Affairs (OBEMLA)

Includes information on bilingual students in this office of the U.S. Department of Education.
http://ww.ed.gov/offices/OBEMLA/

Teachers of English to Speakers of Other Languages, Inc. (TESOL)

Provides information about the teaching of English in the United States and internationally.
www.tesol.org

Also see Burns, M. S., Griffin, P., & Snow, C. E. (Eds.).

(1999). *Starting out right: A guide to promoting children's reading success.* Washington, DC: National Academy Press. (Pages 165-167 list relevant Internet sites.)

Glossary

Academic Language
"Language used in the learning of academic subject matter in formal schooling contexts; aspects of language strongly associated with literacy and academic achievement, including specific academic terms or technical language, and speech registers related to each field of study" (TESOL, 1997, p. 153). Academic language is frequently contrasted with social language.

Alphabetic Principle
"Knowledge of the alphabetic principle is awareness that written words are composed of letters that are intentionally and conventionally related to phonemic segments of the words of oral language" (Burns, Griffin, & Snow, 1999, p. 147).

Background Knowledge
The skills, knowledge, and attitudes that students bring to a learning situation. Background knowledge may be influenced by students' cultural backgrounds, since what people are expected to know and be able to do varies from group to group.

Bilingual Instruction

"Provision of instruction in school settings through the medium of two languages, usually a native and a second language; the proportion of the instructional day delivered in each language varies by the type and goals of the bilingual education program in which instruction is offered" (TESOL, 1997, p. 153).

Code

"A term that is used instead of language, speech variety, or dialect. It is sometimes considered to be a more neutral term than the others" (Richards, Platt, & Platt, 1992, p. 56).

Cognate

"A word in one language that is similar in form and meaning to a word in another language because both languages are related. For example, English brother and German bruder" (Richards et al., 1992, p. 59).

Cohesion

"The grammatical and/or lexical relationships between the different elements of a text. This may be the relationship between different sentences or between different parts in a sentence" (Richards et al., 1992, p. 62).

Comprehension

"Understanding: Listening comprehension refers to spoken language, reading comprehension refers to written language" (Burns et al., 1999, p. 147).

Constructivism

The notion that a student's prior experience, knowledge, and beliefs influence how he or she interprets experiences and uses new information to develop understanding. In teaching, the emphasis is on how learners build new knowledge using various sources of information, including each other. Constructivist teaching focuses not only on outcomes but also on the learning process.

Decoding Skills

"Skills in translating symbols (e.g., alphabet letters) into recognizable syllables and words" (Burns et. al., 1999, p. 147).

Dialect

A regional or social variety of a language distinguished by pronunciation, grammar, or vocabulary differences. The existence of vernacular and standard dialects reflects social evaluation of language differences (Wolfram, Adger, & Christian, 1999).

Emergent Literacy

"A range of activities and behaviors related to written language including those undertaken by very young children who depend on the cooperation of others and/or on creative play to deal with the material: reading and writing related activities and behaviors that change over time culminating in conventional literacy during middle childhood" (Burns et. al., 1999, p. 148).

English Language Learner (ELL)

"Children or adults who are learning English as a second or additional language. This term may apply to learners across various levels of proficiency in English. ELLs may be referred to as non-English speaking (NES), limited English proficient (LEP), and non-native speaking (NNS)" (Echevarria, Vogt, & Short, 2000, p.198).

English as a Second Language (ESL)

"The field of English as a second language: courses, classes, and programs designed for students learning English as an additional language" (TESOL, 1997, p. 154).

First Language (L1)

A speaker's native or mother tongue.

Fluency (reading)

"Achieving speed and accuracy in recognizing words and comprehending connected text, and coordinating the two" (Burns et al., 1999, p. 148).

Fossilization

"A process ... in which incorrect linguistic features become a permanent part of the way a person speaks or writes a language. Aspects of pronunciation, vocabulary usage, and grammar may become fixed in second or foreign language learning" (Richards et al., 1992, p. 145).

Grapheme

The minimal unit of a writing system.

Homophone

"Words that sound alike but are written differently and ... have different meanings. For example, in English *know* and *no* are pronounced the same. Homophones are sometimes called homonyms" (Richards et al., 1992, p. 168).

Language Minority Student

"A student who comes from a home in which a language other than English is primarily spoken; the student may or may not speak English well" (TESOL, 1997, p. 155).

Language Transfer

"The effect of one language on the learning of another. *Negative transfer* is the use of a native-language pattern or rule that leads to an error or inappropriate form in the target language. *Positive transfer* is transfer that makes learning easier, and may occur when both the native language and the target language have the same form" (Richards et al., 1992, p. 205).

Lexicon

The vocabulary of a language.

Limited English Proficient (LEP)

"A term used to refer to a student with restricted understanding or use of written or spoken English; a learner who is still developing competence in using English" (Echevarria et al., 2000, p. 199).

Linguistic Analysis

"Investigation into the structure and functions of a particular language or language variety" (Richards et al., 1992, p. 214).

Linguistics

"The study of language as a system of human communication" (Richards et al., 1992, p. 215).

Literacy

Activities and behaviors "that include reading, writing, and the creative analytic acts involved in producing and comprehending texts" (Burns et al., 1999, p. 149).

Morphology

"The aspects of language structure related to the ways words are formed from prefixes, roots, and suffixes (e.g., mis-spell-ing) and are related to each other" (Burns et al., 1999, p. 149).

Orthography

"A method of representing spoken language by letters and diacritical marks; spelling" (Burns et al., 1999, p. 149).

Phoneme

"In oral language, the units that combine to form syllables and words (e.g., the phonemes in the standard English words *bit* and *hit* are the same except for the first segment and the word *hint* has one more phoneme than the word *hit*)" (Burns et al., 1999, p. 149).

Phonemic Awareness

"A special kind of *phonological awareness* [defined below] involving the smallest units of oral language, phonemes" (Burns et al., 1999, p. 149).

Phonics

"Instructional practices that emphasize how spellings are related to speech sounds in systematic ways; letter-sound correspondences" (Burns et al., 1999, p. 150).

Phonological Awareness

"Knowing that oral language has a structure that is separate from meaning; attending to the sub-lexical structure (i.e., structure within words) of oral language, e.g., *beg* has one syllable and three phonemes, *egg* has one syllable and two phonemes" (Burns et al., 1999, p. 150).

Primary Language

"First or native language spoken by an individual" (TESOL, 1997, p. 155).

Second Language (L2)

A language learned in addition to the mother tongue. A distinction can be made between second languages and foreign languages. The term *second language* refers to a language that a speaker uses regularly for communication. Usually, speakers learn a second or additional language in a setting where that language is used widely. *Foreign language* usually refers to a language that is studied in a setting where it is not used regularly for communication.

Second Language Acquisition (SLA)

"The processes by which people develop proficiency in a second or foreign language" (Richards et al., 1992, p. 325).

Semantics

"The study of meaning" (Richards et al., 1992, p. 329).

Standard American English

The variety of American English that has the highest social status. See definition of *standard language* below.

Standard Language

"The variety of a language that has the highest status in a community or nation and which is usually based on the speech and writing of educated native speakers of the language. A standard variety is generally used in the news media, described in dictionaries, and taught in schools" (Richards et al., 1992, p. 351).

Syntax

"The aspects of language structure related to the ways in which words are put together to form phrases, clauses, or sentences" (Burns et al., 1999, p. 150).

Total Physical Response (TPR)

A language teaching method involving commands and instructions that require a physical response from the learners, e.g., standing up, closing the door (Richards et al., 1992, p. 385).

References

Boring, M. (1996). *Caterpillars, bugs and butterflies*. Minnetonka, MN: Creative Publishing International.

Burns, M. S., Griffin, P., & Snow, C. E. (Eds.). (1999). *Starting out right: A guide to promoting children's reading success*. Washington, DC: National Academicy Press.

Clair, N. (1998). Teacher study groups: Persistent questions in a promising approach. *TESOL Quarterly, 32*(3), 465-492.

Echevarria, J., Vogt, M., & Short, D. (2000). *Making content comprehensible for English language learners: The SIOP model*. Needham Heights, MA: Allyn and Bacon.

Farndon, J. (1999). *Collecting rocks and crystals*. New York: Sterling.

George, M. (1992). *Volcanoes*. Mankato, MN: Creative Education.

Richards, J. C., Platt, J., & Platt, H. (1992). *Dictionary of language teaching and applied linguistics*. Essex, England: Longman.

Simon, S. (1987). *Icebergs and glaciers*. New York: William Morrow.

TESOL. (1997). *ESL standards for pre-K-12 students*. Alexandria, VA: Teachers of English to Speakers of Other Languages.

Wolfram, W., Adger, C. T., & Christian, D. (1999). *Dialects in schools and communities*. Mahweh, NJ: Erlbaum.